NEGATIVITY IS HARMFUL FOR HEALTH

DISCARD IT LIVE HAPPY LIFE

BY BALDEV BHATIA

CREATE SPACE.COM

I0423275

ABOUT THE BOOK

Negativity is harmful for health –Discard it live happy life. It is said that positivity is purely an internal matter. It has nothing to do with our external circumstances. There is something positive within us which helps us to keep us happy and there is something negative within us which makes us unhappy. Happy living through positivity is nothing more than that of living a normal life free from undue pressures, problems and tensions. If we want to live a happy life then we need to get rid of the negativity within us and above all we must start thinking positive which will not make us unhappy. Negative thinking always complicates the problems and increases unhappiness. Most of us do the fatal mistake of looking outwards for happiness rather than looking inwards.

Think positive, be strong, be bold and be courageous every day. Even if we are having a bad day, think of some good things that may come our way, either later that day, tomorrow, next hour, month, or year. When everything seems to be beyond our control, it's almost too easy for us to slip into the grasp of negativity. To avoid negativity, we must strive to abolish this sort of thinking through the power of thinking positively.
The Art of Positive Thinking is not a complicated kind of art difficult to learn rather a simple art of positive thinking, , eating well, and living well like feeling well. What we

need to do is just to tune up our mind to enjoy every moment of life and let the positive thinking follow us. This is something that needs to be looked into thoroughly. We need to focus on the positive aspects rather than on the negative setbacks. We must remember that good and happy living is the reward of positive thinking. We ought to remember, only the positive thinking can bring happiness in our lives. If we cannot think positively, we cannot live happily. Be our own teacher or adviser we ought to look everything with a positive angle. Let us find something good even in most critical moments of our life and let us make positive thinking the basis of our happy living.

It's a matter of thought that fools worry about the circumstances on which they have no control. Why worry when we cannot change anything or the climate, rather enjoy it whether it's hot, humid, cold, cloudy, foggy and snowy. Let us all keep our internal weather mind body and soul pleasant all the time. A sound and positive happiness is all around. It's not far away from us. If we do not want to live happy, it's up to us. It's our own choice. We must not blame others, nor should we blame our fate or external circumstances. Another thing is that feeling confident affects the way we perceive our situations and how we decide to manage them. Think that by being more optimistic we alter our approaches to situations and take on them in a healthier manner; we think of alternatives and act according to better outcomes. If we think positive it will be positive. It does not say to stick our heads in the soil; rather it says to think positive. Interestingly it does not say feel positive it says think positive and that is the real meaning to remain happy.
Happiness does not come alone, it adds our minds body and soul to remain in constant touch with each other. We have to remove negative thoughts and create and atmosphere to be happy in our lives. There are many fear factors that are

reasoning us to be unhappy and the main reason being that our heart and our feelings which are more susceptible to fear and worry then the mind. Of course we do the worrying in our minds but it is our emotions that are worried not our brains.

When the heart senses the possibility of loss it can start panicking and then uses the mind to worry and many times tries to manipulate the brain in dealing with the fear. The heart desires something and gets excited about it and then it manipulates the mind to assure that it will get it. Although the brain can control the emotions and knowledge precedes all, however when it comes to response time the brain is slower than the emotions. That is which explains why we say or do things and then regret them. Our objective in life should be to train ourselves to wait for the brain to show up before we say or do anything. Fear usually comes from the emotions and thinking positive is something the brain is capable of doing. So always think positive. It would be very hard to tell someone who is worried to be good and happy by feeling positive. But if you tell them to think positive that is something even a worried person can do. We need to use our mind to think positive, to think of a positive outcome. Thinking positive brings positive results in its wake; when you react in a positive way to a negative situation you usually get positive in return. Positive mental attitude is effective in many ways. There are limits to the effectiveness of positive thinking. It is not always enough to change deeply entrenched irrational core beliefs about self, others and the world. When someone does something to us do we think about it in a positive way or in a negative way? Do we try to assume that the person who is not treating us the way we should be treated is themselves in pain and needs our love or do we assume that they just don't like us and therefore we need to respond back in kind? It is therefore a must for us to learn understand and remember that we need to be positive and think positive in the interest of our good happy living.

ABOUT THE AUTHOR

Astrology has stood the test of times ever since it revealed the Mystery and the Mastery of the ancient wisdom of forecasting the influence of the stars on human bodies. The author Baldev Bhatia a renowned and world famous Astrologer has penned several simple books on Astrology- this mysterious subject that reveals the true perception of knowing oneself through the art of prediction.

Professionally the author has put his entire life experience in promoting Astrology in various fields with a view to serve the millions of curious readers of this mystic science with the intension of imparting them the real knowledge of Astrology through various interesting and marvelous scriptures. The Astrologer has been associated with Astrology for the past 45 years and has been practicing Astrology in various forms.

The Author-cum Astrologer has been in touch with general public throughout his life and has been practicing phycology and pubic healing. His intension is to guide his readers to achieve their personal goals with ease that would assist them to overcome all the problems, crises, speed breakers and the unforeseen negatives forces, in their lives so as not to get disheartened or depressed in their lives and finally lead a happy life and peaceful life, after going through this manuscript of "Microscopy of Positive Thinking". More over Mr. Baldev Bhatia the Author is an established writer himself with a sound reputation of being a good Astrologer has put his valuable life experience in promoting positivity among his clients. The author also shares with millions of curious readers the 'Ultimate Knowledge' by letting them know more about themselves in detail and also about their in born positive qualities. Possessed by them and guides them to ward off the negativity in them, just by thinking positive and as how to lead an happy and powerful life.

Without caring for the worries troubling them. The main object of writing this manuscript is to impart the basic knowledge of how to Think Positive, be bold, strong, courageous, and how to throw away the negative forces and become a happy person in life. The author also shares the valuable experience of his life with his readers through his valuable and helpful book. His published books "Microscopy of Astrology", Microscopy of Numerology", Microscopy of Remedies, Microscopy of Happy Living, Microscopy of Transiting Planets five volumes also guide his readers to achieve their personal goals with ease and assists them to overcome all the problems, crises, and the unforeseen negatives forces, in their lives gracefully which guides them not get disheartened or depressed at any stage of life irrespective of all the odds and negative forces troubling them.

His readers have gained good experience going through his useful and purposeful books. His books have made his readers to feel secure, sound and have also encouraged them to face their destiny with immense strength and have also given them the power to face the challenges of this universe with utter confidence zeal and power. The author Baldev Bhatia leads way to Positivity Happiness, and Success, and advices his people suffering from depression and negativity in their personal lives to wake up and lead a good happy and positive life.

After meeting hundreds and hundreds of depressed dejected disappointed and unhappy people from all over the world and people from all walks of life and he being a highly experienced Astrologer and Consultant in Astrology and Numerology felt it necessary to write books on Positive Thinking, Positive Living Happiness, Love, and Peace which could guides his readers to ward of their depression, dejection, hatred and negativity in their lives.

His books have also revealed to his readers to attain positivity in their lives so that they could easily achieve their path of glory to be a positive and happy person and also be a brave strong and courageous human being. His books have given gracefully accepted by the people worldwide. His books have helped the masses to achieve and lead a life full of positivity, boldness, strength, courage happiness that have generated confidence in depressed and dejected people. His books have helped his clients and readers to lead a good, peaceful and positive and happy life by Thinking Positive

His books have been very different from others as they guide and help the readers to strengthen their will power and confidence which the readers have lost in today's world and to encourage his readers and to help them, in all walks of life. The esteem Author finally decided to manuscript the following books in the interest and happiness of the Universal People

PREFACE

Author Baldev Bhatia shares with millions of his curious readers the 'ultimate knowledge' by letting them know more about themselves in detail through their born qualities along with, the help of the positive thinking, possessed by them and to ward off the negativity prevailing in them and also get to know the ways as how to live a good and happy life. The worries adopted by them, the negative forces influencing them, need to be discarded for a positive good and happy living by thinking positively. The negative forces influencing the masses, with their negative thoughts has lured the author to pen down the wonders of this mystic manuscript and to bring to the millions of readers the 'real knowledge' by letting them know more about themselves in detail. With the help of astrological science they can come to know more about their Zodiac Signs, the ultimate Remedies required to be done to ward off the negativity in them and to know more about their characteristics; appearances; their personality; profession, career; business, finances, their match with other zodiac signs; romance, marriage, weakness their health and disease and finally the negative forces, if any. Possessed by them and to ward of this negativity factor with the guidance of this manuscript charming them to become more positive so that they can lead a happy life. This Microscopy of Positive Thinking is based on the practical experience of the author who has meet several thousand people having negativity in their personal lives and those leading a miserable life totally being depressed and dejected. The main purpose of writing this manuscript is to impart the basic knowledge of how to become bold, strong, courageous, and how to throw away the negative forces in them. This manuscript reveals a whole lot of information when one is in search for the truths of a positive attitude and positive thinking..

With this the author shares his experience with his readers. His published books "Microscopy of Astrology", Microscopy of Numerology", Microscopy of Remedies", "Microscopy of Happy Living" "Microscopy of Transiting Planets Vol-1, 2, 3, 4, and 5 also guides his readers to achieve their personal goals with ease and assist them to overcome all the problems, crises, and the unforeseen negatives forces, in their lives so as to avoid getting disheartened or depressed and neglected. This book goes to reveal, ascertaining the real facts of life and the destiny as to what is stored for each and every reader in his or her future.

Various chapters have been covered and maximum emphasis have been paid to cover the subjects pertaining to the significance of positivity by reading different charts; different Zodiac signs, planets and their placements in different houses and signs; affliction of planets with the interpretation of the major period and the meaning of the birth signs of the individual birth signs. Author and Astrologer Baldev Bhatia have put his entire life experience in promoting positivity among his clients through this mystic science of Astrology.

He has done so in order to serve millions of curious readers with a good intension of imparting them the basic knowledge of how to become a ward of negative thinking and become a positive person in life.

The author-cum astrologer has been associated with general public for the past 45 years and has been practicing phycology and pubic healing.

His intension is also to guide the readers to achieve their personal goals with ease and would assist them to overcome all the problems, crises, speed breakers and the unforeseen negatives forces, in their lives as not to get disheartened or depressed in their lives.

The Author's main object and message, through this manuscript to his readers is to spread, Peace, Love happiness to the entire world and tries to guide his readers to ward off negativity, depression, dejection and hatred among them. He has done his best to reveal to his readers to attain positivity in way or manner irrespective of all the hardships and to attain a path of glory by getting away from their weakness of negative thinking which should be discarded forever the depression dejection by way of adopting a positive attitude to be bold to be strong and to be courageous, through which they can lead a positive good happy and prosperous life.

This book also intends to guide the readers to achieve their personal goals with ease that would assist them to overcome all the problems, crises, speed breakers and the unforeseen negatives forces, in their lives, as not to get worried or disheartened or depressed or dejected and also not to fall prey to the negative thinking in their lives if the influence of the Transiting Planets is weak, disgusting depressing, unfavorable or disappointing.

This books goes to emphasis that if the influence of the transiting planets is good, it goes on to bring good or positive thinking and better changes or events in life. But if the influence is negative it leads to gives undesired results and negative thinking.

One needs to understand that no matter what aspect a transiting planet makes to natal planets, the individual need to hold on his nerves to be bold to be strong and to have a positive thinking in life whatever be the circumstances governing his future with the positive energy already stored in him. . The chapters in the book are very useful, purposeful, and a pin point to the service of mankind. He wishes success for all his readers.

The author would definitely like to express my sincere thanks to Ms. Alpa Shah Director, Travel Company of UK, for helping and encouraging him to pen down this book in the interest of depressed and dejected and the so called Negative persons of this universe. The author is also grateful and thankful to the publishers for publishing this book.

CHAPTER 1
POSITIVITY

Thought which are provoking our mind, about the uncertainties and the negativities, as to what will happen tomorrow. Worries that are prevailing in our minds are repetitive thoughts associated with feelings of anxiety in anticipation of some negative future event. Whether the worries are about financial crisis, family problems, work, health or any topic of concern, the anxious feelings produced and sustained by the imaginary thoughts which always distinctly appear to be unpleasant. Worrying will carry tomorrow's load with today's strength. Worry will not empty tomorrow of its sorrows, it empties today of its power and strength. Worries make you to move into tomorrow ahead of time. Half the worry in the world is caused by people trying to make decisions before they have sufficient knowledge on which to base a decision. Why worry about the future. Just imagine as to what if we just acted like everything was easy and there was nothing very serious about it to come in future. Worry often gives a small thing a big shadow and its surrounding do frightened with more scary things. Why worry about tomorrow; concentrate on today happening as for tomorrow will worry about itself. Each day has its own worries and troubles.

If there is not any solution to same problem, then do not waste time worrying about it. And if there is a solution to the problem then why waste time worrying about it. Worry will never rob tomorrow of its sorrows, but will only deny today of its meaning happiness and joys. Worrying is actually a form of superstition and creates false images in our mind and that is the main reason and cause which makes and leads us to this point of imagination. A human being can survive almost anything, as long as he or she sees the end in sight.

If something bad or good is to happen it is sure to happen, whether we worry or not. Let us put our energy into today and stop worrying about the future and past. We should not foresee trouble, or worry about what may never happen as past is dead and gone forever and future is uncertain and yet to come. The basic facts we should know about worry. The basic techniques to analyze worry and how to break the worry habit before it breaks us.

These are the simple ways where we can concentrate and get rid of worries prevailing in our thoughts. Annalise worry to see and get the reasons and facts of worry. To avoid reoccurrence of worries, concentrate on prayers as prayers are the best source of remedies of the prevailing worries. The more you pray, the less you'll panic.

The more you worship, the less you worry. There is nothing that wastes the body like worry, and anyone who has any faith in God should need not to worry about anything whatsoever is to happen in future. We ought to know the basic fundamental of analyzing worries. Worries create unnecessary thoughts and these are caused by people going in for unwanted decisions, fore hand not even knowing as to when a good decision is made and not even having sufficient knowledge about it. We must first study and after carefully weighing all the facts than only come to a powerful decision. Simply making castles in the air won't solve our problems but add more to our vows. Anxiety and worry can go hand in hand. When anxiety grabs the mind, it is self-perpetuating.

Your mind gets clogged with numerous with buts and ifs. Do not worry about your life. Worries are repetitive thoughts associated with feelings of anxiety in anticipation of some negative future event. Yet anxious feelings and the worries that lead to them can prove helpful.

It becomes a difficult problem if you are constantly anxious as it will become a hindrance to your everyday life, rather than motivate you to some good and better things. Never worry alone.

Worrisome thoughts reproduce faster so one of the most powerful ways to stop the spiral of worry is simply to disclose the worry to a friend. What you will eat or drink; or about your body, what you will wear. If you know that the circumstance is beyond your control or power change than revise it to your liking. Just try to put a stop-less order on your worries. Don't permit little things which become insects of life to ruin your happiness. Co-operate with the inevitable. Decide just how much anxiety a thing may be worth and refuse to give in anymore. All the happiness is not given in one go it comes slowly and slowly.

If your worries center around, an important relationship in your life, pay special attention to remain positive and be happy. To keep yourself happy, treat your worried thoughts as valuable signals. How to keep from worrying about criticism? Simply unjust criticism is often a disguised compliment. It often means that you have aroused jealousy and envy. Let's keep a record of the fool things we have done and criticize ourselves. The utmost cause of worry is your state of depression. Worries are there to motivate information-gathering and problem-solving. Depression is the inability to construct a future. Depression is inertia. That's the thing about depression:

But depression is so insidious, and it compounds daily, that it's impossible to ever see the end. Depressed people think they know themselves, but maybe they only know depression. There are no hopeless than this to get depressed. Our attitude towards suffering and depression becomes very important because it can affect how we cope with suffering when it arises. Depression is nourished by a lifetime of un grieved and unforgiven causes. Never worry about your heart till it stops beating. How can you deal with anxiety? You might try what when you did. A person worried so much that he decided to hire someone to do his worrying for him. Times will change for the better when you change. Worry is a misuse of the imagination.

Worry is most often a prideful way of thinking that you have more control over life and its circumstances than you actually do. To keep yourself happy, treat your worried thoughts as valuable signals. These are the fundamental facts you should be familiar about worries. A huge factor to stay happy is to cater your worries around, an important relationship in your life and pay special attention sustaining positive relationships. Worries are there to motivate information gathering and problem-solving.

Make your mind firm and do come to a positive decision as come what we will not allow the worries to entire our mind and soul. Once a decision is carefully reached we should get busy carrying out our decisions and should not bother about all the anxieties that are about to come.

When we, or any of our colleagues or associates, are about to worry about a problem, we must write it out and think of the following questions: Instead of worrying about what people say of you, why not spend time trying to accomplish something they will admire. What if we just acted like everything was easy? How would your life be different if you stopped worrying about things we can't control and started focusing on the things we can? Let today be the day.

CHAPTER 2

WHAT DO YOU GET OUT? OF BEING NEGATIVE?

You may feel largely uncomfortable, when worries attack your thoughts and mind which makes worrying about a situation an easier option to get depressed and diffused. While you are consuming more worries you are far too busy to do anything else to fix the real problem and would rather find it hard to get into a smart solution. Thus resulting in a fact that you spend your evenings worrying only without even bothering to find some time to search a new job. You get nothing out of worrying except only to think and cry. Another cause of getting worried is the attachment with which your inner soul gets attracted to. Attachment brings worry. If you have a problem and you come up with the answer, you stop worrying immediately. Our minds can be dishonest, persuading us that we are worrying about something, when our deepest fear is entirely different. No-one likes to admit that they've chosen to worry. The first step is to write down your worries, which will help you make sense of them, and then decide on one small step you can take towards a solution. But to be very true no man in this world is free of obstacles or difficulties.

Don't make worry your habit. Break this habit and stop all the negative and panic thoughts provoking your mind all the time. If you can't change the past, but you must not ruin the present by worrying about the future. Joy is what happens to us when we allow ourselves to recognize how good things really are. When we feel worried and depressed, we need to consciously form a smile on our faces and act upbeat until the happy feeling becomes genuine reality. Feelings of depression and hopelessness and or anger are even tougher to cope with on a consistent basis. When you are worried, you not only hurt yourself, but the limited support systems that are still holding on your mind but making you to get more and more worried and nothing is achieved in terms of success except the re-carnation of worries and worries your actions breed confidence and courage. If you want to conquer fear, anger and worry do not sit ideal and just think about it. Let our deep worrying become advance thinking and planning. If you look into your own mind and heart, and you find nothing wrong there, what is there to worry about? Practically nothing what is there to fear about and again nothing? So why worry unnecessarily and make your present and future dark. Why being a negative person and what do you get out of it being a depression dejected and sad man.?

Why not turn your thoughts to be a positive person simply it is a question of tilting your mind towards a positive side of thing. See both the aspects of a situation and ways the pros and cons of both the sides and try to abolish the negativity in you. Think of the best the best is sure to happen and if you think of the worst the worst will come. Better come forward wake up and think positive first. Positive persons always succeed in life whatever be the circumstances and the negative often dig a death trap for themselves. So why be a negative person why you have all the qualities of being a positive man.

CHAPTER 3

CREATE HAPPINESS WITHIN YOU

If you are interested in getting more happiness, focus on all the ways as if you have already attained success. You need to focus on the thing and create a live within you. If you want love and affection, focus on all the people and the abundance of love that you have to give to them. If we want to have greater health, focus on all the ways that we are healthy, thus creating and delivering a good life within you. You need to admit that there are problems that you cannot change. But you can change the way of your thinking if you identify the main reason of the problem. And if you acknowledge the facts, that you have been negative or inactive in finding a solution to the problem, probably this will make it easier for you to become positive thus creating a new lease of life within you. You must try to make goals. Making goals can give you a more positive outlook on life. People often tend to get bored with life and get the feeling that they are stuck to negative things which the result they often get the feeling of being depressed. Setting a direction for yourself and a goal would surely help you to move forward. If you expecting to succeed, and are not afraid of failure, you have the best chance of staying positive and can create a very positive life within you.

When you, or any of your associates, are tempted to worry about a problem, write out the solution and a definite answer to it. This helps a positive feeling to generate within you. Another thing you need to understand is that there are several ways to cultivate a mental attitude that can bring you peace and happiness and can carnage a good life within you. More of it if you fill your mind with thoughts of peace, courage, health, and hope, your life will be easy to live. You would get a happy feeling of life and mind If you let yourself to forget your own unhappiness, by trying to create a little happiness for others. You are best to yourself. The perfect way to conquer worry is the Prayer of God. To keep yourself from worrying about criticism, do not even try to get mixed with your enemies, because if you do you will hurt yourself far more than we hurting them. Instead of worrying about ingratitude, let's expect it. Let's remember that the only way to find happiness is not to expect gratitude, but to give for the joy of giving. Let us build a happy life within us….generate peace and a healthy atmosphere around us. This will help us to lead a peaceful happy and prosperous life and we would find ourselves to be happier than before. You should do things in the order of their importance. You need to clear your desk of all papers except those relating to the immediate problem at hand.

When you face a problem, solve it then and there, if you have the facts to make a decision. Make a decision fast and do not linger on. Learn to organize, deputize, and supervise and straight away come to decision. Simply postponing it would spoil your good thoughts and there is every

likelihood your mind may get into negative
activities and start thinking in negative manner.
Therefore, write down a list of things that make
you excited, however big, small, likely or unlikely.
Then work to make them occur more often. Look
for moments of joy and savor them. Recognize
your good happening every day. Eat well do plenty
of exercise and do not skip meals It is a known fact
that Physical exercise is known to stimulate our
veins and get to strengthen our minds that lift
depression and anxiety so we need to walk, swim,
run or whatever we like doing best. Those who
create or those who do well on the worst scenario,
give themselves worry and stress, tend to be
devastated. If we cannot get some sunshine, we
can always lighten up our rooms with brighter
lights. We can have lunch outside the office. Take
frequent walks instead of driving our cars over
short distances. No man is indispensable. First of
all our circle of friends is always there to give us
some moral support. Spending time and engaging
ourselves in worthwhile activities could give us a
very enjoyable and satisfying feeling.

Nothing feels better than having group support.
Good friends are quite important and their
company generally lightened up our spirits. To get

to know and to find such friends we simply have to be friendly with ourselves, and then the friendships will naturally follow us. We need to understand the power of touch and support and we have not to underestimate it strength and support. Don't we feel so good when someone pats us on our back and gives us some words of encouragement during your most challenging times and difficult times. Just hug or embrace someone someday you will see that you have almost changed his life. Get intimate with him and try to establish close ties with his family and friends. The love and care expressed by you will tremendously boost him and well as your immune system and fury of worry will be diminished for all. In our lives storms may come and go in the form of reversals, but if we have the power and foundation of inner fulfillment and if we deal with it with a very clear practical mind these storms will not kill us or will not disrupt us. There could be numberless reasons for which we keep on worrying. We may be worried about our health, wealth, loved ones, friends, the happening f yesterday and the follow happenings of tomorrow, the environment or the world politics, but these can be dealt with firm mind and fearless worry if we generate within ourselves the power of enlightenment within ourselves.

CHAPTER 4

POSITIVITY IS STATE OF MIND

Positivity is something you cannot earn or buy. If you have spent your life trying to get some happiness or something that will make you happy, odds are that you are wasting a really good life that you don't know you have. You passed up and overlooked a lot of personal happiness. You are probably spending so much time chasing and dreaming of unnecessary thing of what could be of no use to you and that you are forgetting about all the small and big things occurring right now that could make you happy. People and things alone, won't make you happy. Your own efforts not to get worried or depressed make you happy. You know the saying, that "Positivity is a state of mind". And state of mind is what you think do and act in a peaceful manner without being getting worried or depressed. The best thing about happiness is that you get it is free. You don't have to pay or you do not have to open any account to be happy. You don't have to pay monthly rent for it either. You just have to change your perspective, your views on what you are seeing and feeling. Happiness is not something which is quite readymade. It comes from your own actions and deeds.

Don't let one cloud darken the whole sky.
Angriness and happiness don't mix. You must dig
out the angriness in you, and see that the happiness
has shown and seeded a place to grow its roots.
The ultimate goal of life should be to get happiness
and not get involved into unnecessary worries
falling in the death trap of defeats and failures. The
essence of life is not in the great victories and
grand failures, but in the simple joys. The purpose
of our lives is to be happy. Laugh when you can,
apologize when you should, and let go of what you
can't change. Think positive and just visualize that
what is stored in destiny would not be negative. If
you want to be happy, be positive first practice
meditation. If you want, others to be happy
practice compassion. Whoever is happy will make
others happy, too. Let us be very sure and let us
keep in mind that happiness doesn't depend on any
superficial conditions, it is governed by our mental
attitude only. Our greatest gift to others is to be
happy and to radiate our happiness to the entire
world. Happiness is a guide to direction, not a
place to hide. As a happy person, you radiate
happiness to the world. Visualize your light
radiating throughout the world, passing from
person to person until it encircles the globe.
Resolve to keep happy, and your joy and you shall

form an invincible host against difficulties. The positive persons often dance to the happy tunes of their lives.

The path to happiness is forgiveness of everyone and gratitude for everything. Happiness fills your heart each day and your whole life through with clean thoughts. Any day would be a wonderful day if you do not to take life so seriously. Happiness is not about being a winner -it's about being gentle with life being gentle within you. Happiness blooms in the presence of self-respect and the absence of ego. Love yourself. Love everyone around you. Love everyone in the whole world. When you're feeling depressed or anxious, close your eyes and try to visualize a guided positive imaginary thing. First breathe deeply and relax. How important it is to consistently reach for positive, uplifting, inspirational thoughts. Thought that promote aliveness and abundance. Thoughts that make you feel good. Look at the birds of the air; they do not sow or reap or store away in barns, and yet our heavenly Father feeds them. Imagine that you're already a positive person and you love life. The only thing between us and our desire, to be happy, is one single fact: we are not happy because we often fall into the death trap of depression and wholly because of our negative thoughts. Absence of positive thinking, has eluded us of our great happiness and left us far behind. This very little known fact has kept many of us from reaching our goal of happiness. If you keep thinking things like as if your life is dead!", nothing would be achieved and it will be like that only. Throw away all your negative thoughts and worries, concentrate on the goals to be achieved, on the ray of happiness in you and make sure that you are not falling again into the path of negativity. "Happiness is a state of mind only and not the thoughts of negatives, and it quite true that happiness can only be achieved if you have a positive mind and a clear attitude of being a positive person. Happiness and positivity go hand in hand. If you are positive, you are a happy person and if you possess negativity you would land yourself to be a very negative person thus ruining your life for what of nothing.

CHAPTER 5

DISCARD NEGETIVITY AND BE POSTIVE

You may also feel that life has become terrible for you to live and you are carrying no hope that someone would be there to rescue you. Happiness is your own choice and decision. Each of us can be as happy as we make up our minds to be. We can, if we want, fill up our days with positive attitude chatter and laughter. To be happy, we need to concentrate only on happy thoughts. The ghosts of the past have to be exorcised. You may be working in any field, the key to success is your outlook. Sometimes you may think that no road is left for you from where you can achieve the happiness of life.

There may be chances that someone who was there with you before might hold on to you when you are on the dark side of the life. The experience has taught us that we should buy some strength, hope and positive ness from our loved ones to help ourselves in such a situation rather than surrendering as life is a precious gift of God and is equipped with full of joy and happiness if we help ourselves in these critical moments and live with considerable optimism. Happiness in life comes through the doors of positive thoughts; we do not even realize which one is left open.

We have so many reasons to cry and at the same time plenty of reasons to smile as well. Keeping our dreams and hope alive might be a reason that success and happiness will come our way again. We ought to know that happiness alone does not stand for anything, but it is on our way of thinking that how do we keep ourselves happy in life. Ending up our lives does not lead us to our destination but of course proves we are supposed to be cowards who know not to unfold the doors of belief in God and in ourselves. Failure and disappointment are part of our life. The only thing is that we need to face and solve the problem.

We must not forget to believe in God whatever our situation may be, we would be taken away from Him by the difficulties, in order that we bow down and surrender. But if our faith is strong enough we will not be let down, rather we would break the knees of sorrows and force it to die and lead happy lives. We should not surrender but must find out ways to come out of our worries, anxieties and difficulties. We ought not to indulge ourselves into the darkness of the room but find out the doors to free ourselves from unnecessary fear and worries. We must belief in ourselves and our hearts, and believe in the ones who love us and not the ones whom we love. We must not fall on the negative side of a thing. It is the real time when you keep on revealing the truth of our lives and relations, do not fall on the reverse side but think how good it was that because of the hard times of our lives we could well judge about them. We should always try to be positive and should think that whatever is happening, it is the positive side or consequence of that incident in would be on the positive side of our imagination. With all these thoughts, I would request my readers to implement some good thoughts in their life that would make things easier to be tackled by them. We should accept the situation and fight it with more determination.

In this world nothing is good or bad and only thinking makes it so. We ought to know that advice from people around us will help us to overcome from the any drastic situation. Also we have to always minimize the stress as it gives nothing but takes away joy and happiness from our lives. And finally we need to take things casually and fight with it seriously. The next morning after all, will surely come with fresh air to breathe the new hopes in us with the brightness of the sun.

A clear minded person looks for good qualities in the other person, whereas a negative mind always looks for the fault in the other person, whereas a negative mind always looks for the fault. An optimist goes forward keeping in mind the past, a pessimist thinks of the future and reverts back to the past. In fact negative thoughts are our greatest enemies. Experience the happiness in all circumstances by maintaining better relationships. How about understanding that sadness cannot touch a person with a positive attitude? The capability increases as It boosts up patience and confidence. It increases the decision of making power. Creative way of thoughts appears in the mind. Positive thoughts teach the art of finding solutions to any problem.

Optimism is something what we do. Anxiety and other negative emotions are known to be detrimental to the body, especially to our immune systems, and having an optimistic nature seems to protect against those effects. People who are supposed to be optimistic, about their future, behaving differently.

CHAPTER 6

HAVE POSITVE ATTITUDE

Never let life's hardships disturb you .no one can avoid problems, not even saints or sages. As with any habit, the habit of remaining positive in all situations takes practice and a commitment to yourself to take control. If you tend to think positive you stand to gain all the amenities of a happy life. Positive Thinking leads you to a happy life one must not forgot the life is what you make it, so make it a happy one!. Don't worry on things that may not happen, life is too short to worry too much. Smile and be happy. Make yourself to be positive person. Don't hold onto anything that bothers your mind. It can only hurt your health and it won't help your problems at all. The people that live the longest in this world do not hold grudges or hold or fall prey into negative feelings. Visualize your worries on a large chalkboard in your mind. Watch yourself take a big eraser and erase the problems. Every time the thoughts come back into your head, see yourself with the eraser again. Keep your slate clean and form a habit of thinking positive. We must not worry about tomorrow, for tomorrow will worry about itself. Each day has enough trouble of its own.

Do not anticipate trouble, or worry about what may never happen. Keep in the sunlight. Imagine every day to be a positive day and the last of a life surrounded with hopes,. The hours that come unexpectedly will be much the more grateful. The mind that is anxious about future events is miserable. Present fears are less than horrible imaginings. Positive thinking is sure to ward of every odd imagination and sure to make you a happy person. Positive thinking actually means approaching life's challenges with a positive outlook.

It does not necessarily mean avoiding or ignoring the bad things; instead, it involves making the most of potentially bad situations, trying to see the best in other people, and viewing yourself and your abilities in a positive light. Positive thinking centers on such things as a belief in your abilities, a positive approach to challenges, and trying to make the most of bad situations. Bad things will happen. Sometimes you will be disappointed or hurt by the actions of others. This does not mean that the world is out to get you or that all people will let you down. Instead, positive thinkers will look at the situation realistically, search for ways that they can improve the situation, and try to learn from their experiences. Positive attitude bring good cheer, remembering that the misfortunes hardest to bear are those that never happen, focus on the positive aspects of lives, rather than on the negative setbacks. Let us not waste our lives in doubts and fears. It is not work that kills us, it is worry and the negative thinking. Work is healthy; but worry is rust upon the blade. It is not movement that destroys the machinery, but friction. We need to forget the most disturbing negative thinking in our lives and opt for the positive attitude by following the principles of positive thinking. Not only can positive thinking impact your ability to cope with stress and your immunity, it also has an impact on your overall well-being.

CHAPTER 7

WHY ARE YOU NEGATIVE?

You may feel largely uncomfortable, when worries attack your thoughts and mind which makes worrying about a situation an easier option to get depressed and diffused. While you are consuming more worries you are far too busy to do anything else to fix the real problem and would rather find it hard to get into a smart solution. Thus resulting in a fact that you spend your evenings worrying only without even bothering to find some time to search a new job. You get nothing out of worrying except only to think and cry. Another cause of getting worried is the attachment with which your inner soul gets attracted to. Attachment brings worry. If you have a problem and you come up with the answer, you stop worrying immediately. Our minds can be dishonest, persuading us that we are worrying about something, when our deepest fear is entirely different. No-one likes to admit that they've chosen to worry. The first step is to write down your worries, which will help you make sense of them, and then decide on one small step you can take towards a solution. But to be very true no man in this world is free of obstacles or difficulties.

Don't make worry your habit. Break this habit and stop all the negative and panic thoughts provoking your mind all the time. If you can't change the past, but you must not ruin the present by worrying about the future. Joy is what happens to us when we allow ourselves to recognize how good things really are. When we feel worried and depressed, we need to consciously form a smile on our faces and act upbeat until the happy feeling becomes genuine reality. Feelings of depression and hopelessness and or anger are even tougher to cope with on a consistent basis. When you are worried, you not only hurt yourself, but the limited support systems that are still holding on your mind but making you to get more and more worried and nothing is achieved in terms of success except the re-carnation of worries and worries your actions breed confidence and courage. If you want to conquer fear, anger and worry do not sit ideal and just think about it. Let our deep worrying become advance thinking and planning. If you look into your own mind and heart, and you find nothing wrong there, what is there to worry about? Practically nothing what is there to fear about and again nothing? So why worry unnecessarily and make your present and future dark.

Why being a negative person and what do you get
out of it being a depression dejected and sad man.?
Why not turn your thoughts to be a positive person
simply it is a question of tilting your mind towards
a positive side of thing. See both the aspects of a
situation and ways the pros and cons of both the
sides and try to abolish the negativity in you.
Think of the best the best is sure to happen and if
you think of the worst the worst will come. Better
come forward wake up and think positive first.
Positive persons always succeed in life whatever
be the circumstances and the negative often dig a
death trap for themselves. So why be a negative
person why you have all the qualities of being a
positive man.

CHAPTER 8

BE HAPPY KEEP SMILING

The secret of successful and happy life lies in keeping ourselves smiling and the character which is the foremost important reason that lies within us. Do not be curious about anything, but in everything, by prayer and petition, with thanksgiving, present your requests to God. Whenever your mind is tempted to jump the fence and start to worry, say this verse aloud or to yourself. You may even have to repeat it over and over again.

Steps for a successful and happy life.

Being a positive thinker is not about ignoring reality in favor of aspirational thoughts. It is more about taking a proactive approach to your life. Instead of feeling hopeless or overwhelmed, positive thinking allows you to tackle life's challenges by looking for effective ways to resolve conflict and come up with creative solutions to problems.

Life is not a bed of roses.

Life is a battle field and not a bed of roses as every man on earth has to struggle very hard in making his life happy. If aim of our life is to stay happy and let others to be happy, we will be happy and remembered by all. But no one will actually remember us for the wealth we have gained, or success we have achieved. If we have no aim in life, we would not be able to lead and happy life. Living with no purpose in life is just like a feather moving towards the wind. Both career and purpose are different issues but it is equally important to understand the value of these things which would ultimately add spicy flavor to your living.

Innovation at work place is what is it necessary how well we judge our work, how good we like and enjoy it. If we take our work as a stiff challenge and as learning everyday then we would start loving it and giving our best. However, if we just work for the sake of then nothing is realized and we do not remain happy in life.

We should not aim to have negative thoughts at all.

Now let's us imagine that we are not feeling at our best today, and we are having thoughts that could be classified as negative. We shouldn't be thinking such negative thoughts. We don't like the negative thoughts. We ought to know that negative thoughts are stressful, demoralizing and depressing. We shouldn't aim to have negative thoughts at all. Often we feel uncomfortable because we think we have to say or do something in response to another person's words. When we find ourselves thinking this way, it helps enormously to take a few moments to check inside and notice what we are feeling. Negative thoughts destroy our happy livings. We ought to discard all these negative thought and act to live in a more positive atmosphere rather than living in a negative world where we can never find a happy living.

Happy living allows us to tackle life's challenges

We fall into the trap of unnecessary worries and elope ourselves with negative thoughts. We feel better when somebody else is facing some difficulty but when it comes to us we fail to gather that faith, will power and the words of strength.

Being a positive thinker is not about ignoring reality in favor of aspirational thoughts. It is more about taking a proactive approach to our lives.

Instead of feeling hopeless or overwhelmed, positive thinking allows us to tackle life's challenges by looking for effective ways to resolve conflict and come up with creative solutions to problems. It might not be easy, but the positive impact it will have on our mental, emotional, and physical health will be well-worth it. It takes practice; lots of practice. This is not a step-by-step process that we can complete and be done with. Instead, it involves a lifelong commitment to looking inside ourselves and being willing to challenge negative thoughts and make positive changes. It is a common fact that no one in this world is free of obstacles or difficulties. If all the openings of happiness are shut for us and we have to overcome that and have no way to come out, but to survive lest we must have to learn to swim out of the sorrows because this is what is called life and sorrow free living. There are lot more examples and in many other situations, where we will find that how we could have faced and fought with our sorrows and difficulties of life when there was no hope left in our lives. As commonly said by big saints that the self- seeking man who is looking after his personal comforts and leading a lazy life for himself there would be no room for him even in the hell and he simply have lost the power of his will and he cannot lead a happy life.

The secret of every successful man is to have, good confidence

The secret of every successful man is to have, good confidence, faith and strength behind him and that remain the right cause of his single success in life. Unselfishness plays a very vital role in his life. He may not have been perfectly unselfish, yet he was tending towards it. If he had been perfectly unselfish, he would have been as great a success.

The degree of unselfishness marks the degree of success everywhere and he leads to be successful man without fear worries and selfishness. Therefore creation of positivity in life is utmost necessary to enjoy the special gift of God to us. The love for God and worshipping God adds to one common thing the immense faith in Him. There may be different beliefs and ways to worship God in different communities, places and religions, but one thing remains the same and that is the Love of God for all of us. Our world is full of odds and evens, happiness and sorrows, fulfilment and emptiness. And these are all created by the Almighty. However, the most beautiful Gift of God, is Human, which is such a mystery driven by Him which could hardly be defined or explained in depth.

If aim of our life is to stay happy and let others to be happy, we will be happy and remembered by all.

We know that life cannot be foreseen. Life is not a bed of roses. Life is a battle field and not a bed of roses as every man on earth has to struggle very hard in making his life happy. But no one will actually remember us for the wealth we have gaincd, or success we have achieved until and unless we do not live a happy life. Life is such a special gift of Almighty and it is not gifted by Him to use it the way we like or love to. The actual path shown by Him needs to be followed by us for us to reach the peak of betterment every moment.

We need to have some positive attitude to look at it comfortably but at the same time having a positive mental attitude does not mean banishing all negative thoughts and people from your life. We need to believe that a positive attitude is a choice. This step is hard to take. People are either positive or negative.

They tend to blame their negativity on all kinds of outside forces fate, experiences, parents, relationship, but never really stopped to think that they could choose to be positive. Piercing ourselves that positivity is a choice has been one of the greatest things we have ever done for ourselves. Now when we find ourselves in a bad situation, we know that it's up to us to find the good, to be positive regardless of what's happening around us. We should no longer point fingers and place blame to anyone else. We need to realize that everything happens how it happens, and it's up to us to choose how we want to feel about it. We need to be in control of our attitude, and no one can take that away this from us. If we want to live a positive, joyful and happy life, we must not be surrounded by negative people who don't encourage our happiness. As a negative person, we ought to get attracted too negative people only. Only when we decide to make the change to live a more positive life, we have to get rid of our lives of the most negative influences in it. We are quite aware of the fact that no one is perfect and perfection isn't the goal when it comes to positivity but there were people in our lives who were consistently negative, who constantly bring us down, we need to stop spending so much time with them.

We can very well imagine, it is not easy for us to get away from these negative people.

It can hurt us to keep distance from people even when you know they aren't good for us and for our current lifestyle. In addition to removing negative influences from them, we also have to get rid of some of our own negative behaviors, such as the drug and alcohol abuse. We need to take some concrete steps and examine which behaviors are good for us and which were not harmful. What we need is to learn to focus on the positive things, such as working on positive activities and cultivating new, positive relationships.

We must let go of the negative ones. This process may be not easy to live a positive life when negative people and behaviors continually pull us down. In every situation or in every person there is something good.

Anything good and bad is learning experience.

Most of the time it's not easy to find the positive qualities but we have to look hard to discover positivity in them. Now, when we are faced with a difficult or challenging situation, we need to think and talk to ourselves and console our mind, no matter how terrible the situation might seem, we can always find something good if we take the time to think about it. It is quite obvious that anything good and bad is learning experience so, at the very least, we must learn from bad experiences. However, there's usually even more to it than that. If you really take some time to have a look at it, we would find something good, something genuinely positive, about every person or situation. Not only do we need to be happy with ourselves for this multiple action to take effect, but we also need to be more positive and happy with others. We have to share our wealth of happiness with the people of the world. The best way is to be nice with other people, no matter what. Tell them that they look nice today. Appreciate their job and tell them that have done a great job on that assignment. Be happy and tell your elder or you kid how much you love them and how great they are.

When someone is feeling down, do what we need to do is to cheer him or her up. Do send them gifts nice flower and glow them with nice notes. By doing this we will not make ourselves happy but in turn give and generate happiness for others too. At times we may suffer from chronic depression, though we know how good things look on to others life cannot be worse for us.

Let's imagine how to deal when life leaves a great big steaming pile at our doorstep. Lest we need to remember that external factors can be dealt with by taking positive and happy steps to repair or at least address the root of the problem as best as we can. Whatever may be the primary cause of the problem, that cause must be examined first? What is required is that we never wanted to see the good in ourselves and, therefore, didn't want to see it in others also. We must not be critical and condescending rather we must be encouraging and supportive. We should not try to treat others as we would like to be treated, but also try to consider how we would like to be treated. The world likes to appreciate positivity, and the more we share it with others, the more we would be practicing it your own lives. When we start feeling like the idea of not being a happy person we need to remind ourselves that all it takes is one tiny step in the right direction to move towards a more happy life.

Share your happy thoughts with others

We have to believe in ourselves and remember the most important lesson of all is a happy outlook and that is a choice that we can always make. The power of remaining happy, whatever the situation, can never be underestimated. We are all here for a short duration, but is it worth it to spend any of that time in a any angry or being negative? That need to sort out in mind and soul and thus must share our happy thoughts with others. The real test of any one is to remain happy whenever some challenges become difficult. Remaining happy keeps our mind in the right state of balance and often opens resolutions to the problems at hand. Negativity is contagious and spreads like fire. It not only does its affect anyone, but it spreads to everyone who ever comes in contact with it or whoever they interact with.

When only the negative perspective is in focus, the resolution process is impeded. Eliminating negativity, or rather, being positive is a mindset that can be found at any moment, and which can be turned into a habit. We must throw away the negativity in us and opt for being a very positive person this in turn will make us happy and we would be able to lead a sweet and happy life forever.

CHAPTER 9

WHY NEGATIVE THINKING

At time we may think that there is no road is left for us from where we can achieve the happiness of our lives. We may also feel that life has become terrible for us to live and we are carrying new hope that someone would come to rescue us. There may be chances that someone who was there with us before might have held on to us when we were on the dark side of the life. We should not forget that happiness in life comes through the doors of positive thoughts; we need to have them first.

If one door happens to close, another opens, in the event only when we are confident and optimistic. We have so many reasons to cry and at the same time plenty of reasons to smile as well. Similarly, happiness does not stand for anything, but is on our way of thinking that how do we keep ourselves happy in life.

Failure and disappointment are part of our life. The only thing is that we need to face and solve the problem is by keeping our dreams and hope alive be it a reason that success and happiness will come our way again.

The experience has taught us that we should buy some strength, hope and positivity from our loved ones to help ourselves in such a situation rather than surrendering as life is a precious gift of God And is equipped with full of joy and happiness if we help ourselves in these critical moments we can live with considerable optimism. What if when everything goes wrong and all the doors of happiness are closed our live becomes a silent. It is a quite common and we are aware of a marvelous proverb that Life itself is a stage and we all are the performers, performing different acts assigned to us by our almighty power.

We should not forget as to what is in our possession? if it is to fulfill our duties towards our responsibility and do whatever is correct and is allowed by us in our life?

However, despite of all these good thoughts which are embodied to us by the almighty fail to revive these unwanted circumstances that lead us to sorrow and difficulties and a situation where we do not know what is correct and good for us and what is wrong for us. We should always remember that, "Life is there, where there is hope".

That single thing that remains in our hands is to find out ways to know how to overcome these worries of our life at that very moment when all doors are closed for us which means that whatever situation is there, we must not give up hope. We must fight because there has been always a chance that with good faith and hard work we can turn the odds in our favor. It is often said that it is very easy to advice but when it comes to us, things go out of our control and we fail to suggest a way out for ourselves. We fall into the trap of unnecessary worries and elope ourselves with negative thoughts. We feel better when somebody else is facing some difficulty but when it comes to us we fail to gather that faith, will power and the words of strength. It is a common fact that no one in this world is free of obstacles or difficulties. If all the openings of happiness are shut for us and we have to overcome that and have no way to come out, but to survive lest we must have to learn to swim out of the sorrows because this is what is called life and sorrow free living. There are lot more examples and in many other situations, where we will find that how we could have faced and fought with our sorrows and difficulties of life when there was no hope left in our lives.

When the power of will is at the worst and each one of us knows that the one who is gone never comes back. Neither a thousands of words would not be enough to bring him back nor a million tears, because each and every moment, eyes would only shed tears, mind would remain tensed and we would be simply surrounded by worries and the life seems to have been vanished. Life is ever expanding, contraction is death.

As commonly said by big saints that the self-seeking man who is looking after his personal comforts and leading a lazy life for himself there would be no room for him even in the hell and he simply have lost the power of his will. We are quite aware of the fact that faith in oneself is the history of a man and that faith calls the quality of superiority within a person. One cannot do anything without it. We fail only when we do not try very hard to achieve the power and faith within us. As soon as we lose faith, death comes in our way and we are surrounds by all the evils and stupid worries of the world. The secret and history of every successful man is to have, good confidence, faith and strength behind him and that remain the right cause of his single success in life. Unselfishness plays a very vital role in his life.

He may not have been perfectly unselfish, yet he was tending towards it. If he had been perfectly unselfish, he would have been as great a success. The degree of unselfishness marks the degree of success everywhere and he leads to be successful man without fear worries and selfishness. There are quite a number of reasons to believe that for a successful and happy life the mystery surrounding it lies in our interests, and good memory which is the basis of our interest, power of desire and aim, keeping ourselves smiling and the doubt free character which is the foremost important reason for a successful and happy life.

If we possess one solid unselfish and doubt free character within ourselves we would be quite happy and successful. The love for God and worshipping God adds to one common thing the immense faith in Him. There may be different beliefs and ways to worship God in different communities, places and religions, but one thing remains the same and that is the Love of God for all of us. Our world is full of odds and evens, happiness and sorrows, fulfilment and emptiness. And these are all created by the Almighty. However, the most beautiful

Gift of God, is Human, which is such a mystery driven by Him which could hardly be defined or explained in depth. We know that life cannot be foreseen. Life is not a bed of roses.

Life is a battle field and not a bed of roses as every man on earth has to struggle very hard in making his life happy. If aim of our life is to stay happy and let others to be happy, we will be happy and remembered by all. But no one will actually remember us for the wealth we have gained, or success we have achieved. I have no aim in life. Summary living with no purpose in life is just like a feather moving towards the wind. Both career and purpose are different issues but it is equally important to understand the value of these things which would ultimately add spicy flavor to your living. Innovation at work place is what is it necessary how well we judge our work, how good we like and enjoy it.

If we take our work as a stiff challenge and as learning everyday then we would start loving it and giving our best. However, if we just work for the sake of then nothing is realized and we do not remain happy in life. Life is such a special gift of Almighty and it is not gifted by Him to use it the way we like or love to.

The actual path shown by Him needs to be followed by us for us to reach the peak of betterment every moment. We need to have some positive attitude to look at it comfortably but at the same time having a positive mental attitude does not mean banishing all negative thoughts and people from your life.

The same is true with thoughts. When we go to field with negative thoughts, we banish one and another one arises. Therefore creation of positivity in life is utmost necessary to enjoy the special gift of God to us. Now let's us imagine that we are not feeling at our best today, and we are having thoughts that could be classified as negative. We shouldn't be thinking such negative thoughts. We don't like the negative thoughts. We ought to know that negative thoughts are stressful, demoralizing and depressing. We shouldn't aim to have negative thoughts at all. Often we feel uncomfortable because we think we have to say or do something in response to another person's words. When we find ourselves thinking this way, it helps enormously to take a few moments to check inside and notice what we are feeling. We are deeply depressed that negativity has governed us and has taken a deep root in our minds.

CHAPTER 10

STEPS FOR POSITIVITY

The secret of successful and happy life lies in keeping ourselves smiling and the character which is the foremost important reason that lies within us. Do not be curious about anything, but in everything, by prayer and petition, with thanksgiving, present your requests to God. Whenever your mind is tempted to jump the fence and start to worry, say this verse aloud or to yourself. You may even have to repeat it over and over again. Am I constantly striving to see the positive in every aspect of my life? Steps for a successful and happy life.

Step One:

We need to believe that a Positive Attitude is a choice. This step is hard to take. People are either positive or negative. They tend to blame their negativity on all kinds of outside forces—fate, experiences, parents, relationship, but never really stopped to think that they could choose to be positive. Piercing ourselves that positivity is a choice has been one of the greatest things we have ever done for ourselves.

Now when we find ourselves in a bad situation, we know that it's up to us to find the good, to be positive regardless of what's happening around us. We should no longer point fingers and place blame to anyone else. We need to realize that everything happens how it happens, and it's up to us to choose how we want to feel about it. We need to be in control of our attitude, and no one can take that away this from us.

Step Two:

Get Rid Your Life of Negativity

If we want to live a positive, joyful life, we must not be surrounded by negative people who don't encourage our happiness. As a negative person, we ought to get attracted too negative people only. Only when we decide to make the change to live a more positive life, we have to get rid of our lives of the most negative influences in it. We are quite aware of the fact that no one is perfect and perfection isn't the goal when it comes to positivity but there were people in our lives who were consistently negative, who constantly bring us down, we need to stop .We can very well imagine, it is not easy for us to get away from these negative people.

It can hurt us to keep distance from people even when you know they aren't good for us and for our current lifestyle. In addition to removing negative influences from them, we also have to get rid of some of our own negative behaviors, such as the drug and alcohol abuse. We need to take some concrete steps and examine which behaviors are good for us and which were not harmful. What we need is to learn to focus on the positive things, such as working on positive activities and cultivating new, positive relationships. We must let go of the negative ones. This process may be not easy to live a positive life when negative people and behaviors continually pull us down.

Step Three: Look for the Positivity in Life

In every situation or in every person there is something good. Most of the time it's not easy to find the positive qualities but we have to look hard to discover positivity in them.

Now, when we are faced with a difficult or challenging situation, we need to think and talk to ourselves and console our mind, no matter how terrible the situation might seem, we can always find something good if we take the time to think about it.

It is quite obvious that anything good and bad is learning experience so, at the very least, we must learn from bad experiences. However, there's usually even more to it than that. If you really take some time to have a look at it, we would find something good, something genuinely positive, about every person or situation.

Step Four: Reinforce Positivity in Yourself

Once we start thinking more positively, we will realize that we had to reinforce these thoughts and behaviors within ourselves so that we could stick to it. As with any sort of training, the more we practice, the better we get to be positive. The best and easiest way to do this is to be positive when it comes to who we are. We need to speak to ourselves that we are awesome. And we have done a good job at work thus creating positivity within us. We need to be honest with ourselves, and we need to do our best to look for the good. And, whatever we do, we must not focus on the negative. It is alright not to like everything about ourselves, but don't focus on what we don't like. We have all the positive attributes, and it's up to us to remind ourselves of them every day.

Step Five: Share Positivity with Others

Not only do we need to be positive with ourselves for this multiple action to take effect, but we need to be more positive with others. We have to share our wealth of positivity with the people of the world. The best way is to be nice with other people, no matter what. Tell them that they look nice today. Appreciate their job and tell them that have done a great job on that assignment. Be positive and tell your elder or your kids how much you love them and how great they are.

When someone is feeling down, do what we need to do is to cheer him or her up. Do send them gifts nice flower and glow them with nice notes. What is required is that we never wanted to see the good in ourselves and, therefore, didn't want to see it in others also. We must not be critical and condescending rather we must be encouraging and supportive.

We should not try to treat others as we would like to be treated, but also try to consider how we would like to be treated. The world likes to appreciate positivity, and the more we share it with others, the more we would be practicing it your own lives.

When we start feeling like the idea of not being a positive person we need to remind ourselves that all it takes is one tiny step in the right direction to move towards a more positive attitude. We have to believe in ourselves and remember the most important lesson of all is a positive outlook and that is a choice that we can always make. The power of remaining positive, whatever the situation, can never be underestimated. We are all here for a short duration, but is it worth it to spend any of that time in a any angry or being negative? That need to sort out in mind and soul and thus must share our positive thoughts with others. The real test of any one is to remain positive whenever some challenges become difficult.

'Remaining positive keeps our mind in the right state of balance and often opens resolutions to the problems at hand. Negativity is contagious and spreads like fire. It not only does its affect anyone, but it spreads to everyone who ever comes in contact with it or whoever they interact with. When only the negative perspective is in focus, the resolution process is impeded. Eliminating negativity, or rather, being positive is a mindset that can be found at any moment, and which can be turned into a habit.

We must throw away the negativity in us and opt for being a very positive person.

CHAPTER 11

CREATE HAPPINESS WITHIN YOU

If you are interested in getting more happiness, focus on all the ways as if you have already attained success. You need to focus on the thing and create a live within you. If you want love and affection, focus on all the people and the abundance of love that you have to give to them. If we want to have greater health, focus on all the ways that we are healthy, thus creating and delivering a good life within you. You need to admit that there are problems that you cannot change. But you can change the way of your thinking if you identify the main reason of the problem. And if you acknowledge the facts, that you have been negative or inactive in finding a solution to the problem, probably this will make it easier for you to become positive thus creating a new lease of life within you. You must try to make goals. Making goals can give you a more positive outlook on life. People often tend to get bored with life and get the feeling that they are stuck to negative things which the result they often get the feeling of being depressed. Setting a direction for yourself and a goal would surely help you to move forward.

If you expecting to succeed, and are not afraid of failure, you have the best chance of staying positive and can create a very positive life within you. When you, or any of your associates, are tempted to worry about a problem, write out the solution and a definite answer to it. This helps a positive feeling to generate within you. Another thing you need to understand is that there are several ways to cultivate a mental attitude that can bring you peace and happiness and can carnage a good life within you. More of it if you fill your mind with thoughts of peace, courage, health, and hope, your life will be easy to live. You would get a happy feeling of life and mind If you let yourself to forget your own unhappiness, by trying to create a little happiness for others. You are best to yourself. The perfect way to conquer worry is the Prayer of God. To keep yourself from worrying about criticism, do not even try to get mixed with your enemies, because if you do you will hurt yourself far more than we hurting them. Instead of worrying about ingratitude, let's expect it. Let's remember that the only way to find happiness is not to expect gratitude, but to give for the joy of giving.

Let us build a happy life within us….generate peace and a healthy atmosphere around us. This will help us to lead a peaceful happy and prosperous life and we would find ourselves to be happier than before. You should do things in the order of their importance. You need to clear your desk of all papers except those relating to the immediate problem at hand. When you face a problem, solve it then and there, if you have the facts to make a decision. Make a decision fast and do not linger on. Learn to organize, deputize, and supervise and straight away come to decision. Simply postponing it would spoil your good thoughts and there is every likelihood your mind may get into negative activities and start thinking in negative manner. Therefore, write down a list of things that make you excited, however big, small, likely or unlikely. Then work to make them occur more often. Look for moments of joy and savor them. Recognize your good happening every day. Eat well do plenty of exercise and do not skip meals It is a known fact that Physical exercise is known to stimulate our veins and get to strengthen our minds that lift depression and anxiety so we need to walk, swim, run or whatever we like doing best.

Those who create or those who do well on the worst scenario, give themselves worry and stress, tend to be devastated. If we cannot get some sunshine, we can always lighten up our rooms with brighter lights. We can have lunch outside the office. Take frequent walks instead of driving our cars over short distances. No man is indispensable. First of all our circle of friends is always there to give us some moral support. Spending time and engaging ourselves in worthwhile activities could give us a very enjoyable and satisfying feeling. Nothing feels better than having group support. Good friends are quite important and their company generally lightened up our spirits. To get to know and to find such friends we simply have to be friendly with ourselves, and then the friendships will naturally follow us. We need to understand the power of touch and support and we have not to underestimate it strength and support. Don't we feel so good when someone pats us on our back and gives us some words of encouragement during your most challenging times and difficult times? Just hug or embrace someone someday you will see that you have almost changed his life. Get intimate with him and try to establish close ties with his family and friends.

The love and care expressed by you will
tremendously boost him and well as your immune
system and fury of worry will be diminished for
all. In our lives storms may come and go in the
form of reversals, but if we have the power and
foundation of inner fulfillment and if we deal with
it with a very clear practical mind these storms will
not kill us or will not disrupt us. There could be
numberless reasons for which we keep on
worrying. We may be worried about our health,
wealth, loved ones, friends, the happening f
yesterday and the follow happenings of tomorrow,
the environment or the world politics, but these
can be dealt with firm mind and fearless worry if
we generate within ourselves the power of
enlightenment within ourselves.

CHAPTER 12

HAVE POSTIVENESS IN YOU

We need to remember that as we possibly as we can we should make it a point to eat a more balanced, and healthy diet even though we may very little money left with us. We have intake of lot of greens vegetables and with variety of fruit and nuts which are all super healthy food for us, and which are moreless expensive than meats, cheeses, and processed foods! Their nitrifying value will energize and elevate our body, and knowing this that we are treating ourselves will surely refresh our minds. If we look for rich food rich in vitamins and other useful ingredients which include nuts, soya beans and fatty fish we would get more nutrition value. We must cut back on the caffeine drinks, alcohol. We don't have to quit, but reducing the intake of them will help reduce anxiety and stress from time to time. Exercise is one of health sport that our body needs most. It may be yoga, cross training, or even a simple walking in the park. This helps keeping our body active and will also help to grow our outlook. If we make it hobby, we would enjoy the most.

Whether its art, photography, music focusing on something other than the worry factor it will give our mind some good atmosphere to breathe off and would generate a good behavior within us.

The other refreshing factor is naturally our sleep. We need not be reminded of this. Our body is probably begging us for it when we are in the middle of hard times. We may be drawn to maintain good sleeping habits. Maintain a consistent sleep schedule, but allow yourself some leeway. If we sleep peacefully let our body get about 8 hours of sleep, we get the best results. If you're just starting to have those thoughts, speak to your physician or your therapist. They may prescribe something to help steer you back to the center, emotionally. It may be the act of talking about it is therapeutic enough, but don't assume that. Leave that call to the professionals. Having goals which are set again and again after each one is achieved will give you a mindset or target to strive for which leads to success, with success becomes natural positive attitude. With all costiveness, goals and success builds a higher potential and belief within yourself. Setting realistic goals that you know you can achieve by staying positive is a great beginning to success.

Your attitude around your friends, family and public people really tells them who you are, being positive instead of negative makes an excellent first impression on anybody. Positive means to be absolute, clear-cut, definite, forward-looking and expressively firm with a decision. Having a positive attitude toward something means you are willing to commit and do the work without complaint, which leads to goals. You realize that what appears negative today will change tomorrow. Nothing stays the same. Whether you are positive or negative, the situation does not change. So, we mind as well be positive. As with any habit, the habit of remaining positive in all situations takes practice and a commitment to yourself to take control. But start small, start paying attention to your emotions, start by wanting to change. Communicate each other with positive talks. If you have a problem, the thing to do is to communicate: find out the information you need to get the full picture, so that the solution becomes apparent. If you're upset, you need to communicate and say how you feel. If you've done something wrong, again you need to communicate the nature of this world is that we have to face birth, old age, disease and death. Everything is always changing.

The biggest problem is that we want to control our environment. Don't hold onto anything that bothers your mind. It can only hurt your health and it won't help your problems at all. The people that live the longest in this world do not hold grudges or hold onto negative feelings. Visualize your worries on a large chalkboard in your mind. Watch yourself take a big eraser and erase the problems.

Every time the thoughts come back into your head, see yourself with the eraser again. Keep your slate clean! "Worry does not empty tomorrow of its sorrow, it empties today of its strength. If a problem is fixable, if a situation is such that you can do something about it, then there is no need to worry. If it's not fixable, then there is no help in worrying. There is no benefit in worrying whatsoever." "Worrying is carrying tomorrow's load with today's strength- carrying two days at once. It is moving into tomorrow ahead of time. Worrying doesn't empty tomorrow of its sorrow, it empties today of its strength." "If we are worried about the future, then we must look today at the upbringing of children. Life is what you make it, so make it a happy one!! Don't worry on things that may not happen, life is too short to worry too much. Smile and be happy.

Recent studies have shown that smiling cause's natural body chemicals to increase that can increase your good health. You receive the same benefits whether you feel like smiling or not. Smiling also benefits everyone that sees it. Smiling at others makes them feel good too. So smile, fake or not, it is good for you and good for your recipient. It is the best medicine. Based on the same concept above about smiling, laughing burns calories, increases your adrenaline and boosts health. There are even groups of people that get together just to laugh together. They are not laughing at jokes, they are just laughing for good health. As with smiling, you do not need to laugh at real things, you just need to do the physical laughing for all of the health benefits.

Even small amounts of exercise make you feel better. Take a walk if you are feeling bluesy, angry or think you may be slipping into negative thinking. Getting your blood pumping empowers you to do what you need to do and to do what's right. Set a schedule of regular exercise at least 3 days a week for at least 20 minutes each session for better health. See articles below for starting a fitness program.

Even a little bit helps, if you need to start out small, that is fine, just walk for 10 minutes a day and slowly increase it.

CHAPTER 13

BE POSITIVE

Don't hold onto anything that bothers your mind. It can only hurt your health and it won't help your problems at all. The people that live the longest in this world do not hold grudges or hold onto negative feelings. Visualize your worries on a large chalkboard in your mind. Watch yourself take a big eraser and erase the problems. Every time the thoughts come back into your head, see yourself with the eraser again. Keep your slate clean! Therefore, do not worry about tomorrow, for tomorrow will worry about itself. Each day has enough trouble of its own. Do not anticipate trouble, or worry about what may never happen. Keep in the sunlight. Imagine every day to be the last of a life surrounded with hopes, cares, anger and fear. The hours that come unexpectedly will be much the more grateful. The mind that is anxious about future events is miserable. Present fears are less than horrible imaginings. Let us be of good cheer, remembering that the misfortunes hardest to bear are those that never happen, focus on the positive aspects of their lives, rather than on the negative setbacks.

"Feeling confident affects the way we perceive our situations and how we decide to manage them. Don't waste your life in doubts and fears: spend yourself on the work before you, well assured that the right performance of this hour's duties will be the best preparation for the hours or ages that follow it.It is not work that kills men, it is worry. Work is healthy; you can hardly put more on a man than he can bear. But worry is rust upon the blade. It is not movement that destroys the machinery, but friction. Never let life's hardships disturb you ... no one can avoid problems, not even saints or sages. As with any habit, the habit of remaining positive in all situations takes practice and a commitment to yourself to take control. Life is what you make it, so make it a happy one!! Don't worry on things that may not happen, life is to short to worry to much. Smile and be happy

CHAPTER 14

HAVE POSITIVE THINKING

Have Positive Thinking, think positive as all your thoughts, good and bad, are the creation of your mind which tends to lead you to a materialistic life and go in to generate unnecessary worries. Thus you will learn to be more positive. The environment and all the experiences in your life are the results of your habitual and dominant thoughts. Positive thoughts bring good and happiness. Negative thoughts could tell us about something that needs special attention when they lead us to the path of worries. We must discover what needs to be done, and think positively to take care of it. Many of us fail to see a negative occurrence and do not think of a replacement of negative thought with positive one. As they even do not even dare look for a bright side in every situation. If we do this for a longer period of time, we become habitual, and it will make a tremendous delay in improving our positive thinking skills. We must remember, everything can be framed positively if we make a restless effort to do so. Positive thinking wards off the ingredients of negative thoughts in our minds

There are both positive and negative aspects to most situations. We get to choose which ones we will focus on. We can try to catch ourselves when we're being negative and do not try thinking the positive side of the things. There's no sense in worrying about the negatives if these negatives cannot be changed. If we waste energy and happiness on the things we can't change, we'll only make ourselves more frustrated and come to the stage of depression dejection and disappointments.

Negativity is a habit and we often don't realize we're doing ourselves down. Under each negative thought that we have written, we can spot an alternative way of looking at it, that isn't so negative. Take your mind to positivity and mold and drive your thoughts to the positivity. There's a world of difference between expecting failure or rejection so as not to be disappointed when it occurs and recognizing it as a possibility of being positive. It's sensible to look at a situation from all angles and to have a back-up plan to fall back on if need be. People who do this will not see failure as another step on the road to eventual success; but by expecting and envisioning success, there's less likely to be a failure. Let us find some ways of removing negative thoughts and discouraging our worries to be born.

The first step is by way of giving a good smile.

The easiest way is smiling. Many theories have revealed that even a forced smile can lift one's mood and can divert your mind to positive thinking. We may also share positivity with others by flashing them with a brilliant and good smile. Positive Thinking is a reward of good Smiling and not a risk. The only thing we risk when we think positive is giving ourselves a little more happiness.

The second good step is to have the company of positive thinking friends.

Keep yourself busy and surround yourself with good friends, who always think positive. Appreciate the people in your life who have stood by you through thick and thin. Count their support and analyses the positivity in them which will help you to become more positive, and in the process you will probably help them too.

Good friends help each other in the days of crises and through both the good and bad times. Feel positive about them and feel lucky to have them in your company. Share positive thoughts with them. Tell them to be more positive in live.

The third step is to focus your imagination on positive thoughts

Focus your imagination and make efforts on becoming new positive person. Create positivizes in you. Divert your mind to positive thinking. It is much easier to bring about change if you just put your mind to it and change your thoughts into a much more positive direction. We know that it is difficult for us to control things that happen in our lives, but we can, with some effort, control what we think or do in our lives. Positive thinking will make our imagination livelier and we would be able to lead our lives without many worries. Dejection, Disappointments and Depression, however, has consequences that could ruin our, health, and well-being. This is the reason why many people suffer from depression much more often in winter than in the other seasons. It's because the days are shorter and do not divert their minds to focus to the imagination of positive thinking.

CHAPTER 15

ANALYSING POSITVE THINKING

Negative thought which are provoking our mind, about the uncertainties and the negativities, as to what will happen tomorrow creates unnecessary worries and worries are repetitive thoughts associated with feelings of anxiety in anticipation of some negative future event which may end in a failure. Whether the worries are about financial crisis, family problems, work, health or any topic of concern, the anxious feelings and negative thoughts produced are always distinctly unpleasant. Annalise positive thinking and stop worry over petty matters. Worrying will carry tomorrow's load with today's strength. Worry will not empty tomorrow of its sorrows, but it tends to empty today of its power and strength. Worries make you to move into tomorrow ahead of time. Half the worry in the world is caused by people trying to make decisions before they have sufficient knowledge on which to base a decision. Their negative thoughts pressurize them to be away from the positivity in their lives as they fail and do not analysis on positive

Generate Positive Thinking

Why worry about the future. Just imagine as to what if we just acted like everything was easy and there was nothing very serious about it to come in future. Worry often gives a small thing a big shadow and its surrounding do frightened with more scary things. Why worry about tomorrow; concentrate on today happening as for tomorrow will worry about itself. Each day has its own worries and troubles. Always think positive. If there is not any solution to the some problem then do not waste time worrying about it.

And if there is a solution to the problem then why waste time worrying about it. Act fast be positive generate positive thinking worries will automatically vanish in the air. But if you tend to worry they will never rob tomorrow of its sorrows, but will only deny today of its meaning happiness and joys. Negative thoughts only produce worries and worrying is actually a form of superstition and creates false images in our mind and that is the main reason and cause which makes and leads us to this point of imagination. A human being can survive almost anything, as long as he or she sees the end in sight and starts analyzing his positive thoughts. We must not forgot that ff something bad or good is to happen it is sure to happen, whether we worry or not. Let us put our energy into today and stop worrying about the future and past. We should not foresee trouble, or worry about what may never happen as past is dead and gone forever and future is uncertain and yet to come. Positive Thinking will ward off everything and bring happiness in our lives. The basic facts we should know about worry. The basic techniques to analyze worry and how to break the worry habit before it breaks us. These are the simple ways where we can concentrate and get rid of worries prevailing in our thoughts.

Think Positive and Pray- Why Worry?

Annalise positive thinking by annualizing worry you get to see and get the reasons and facts of worry. To avoid reoccurrence of worries, concentrate on prayers as prayers are the best source of remedies of the prevailing worries.

Think Positive and Pray. The more you pray, the less you'll panic. The more you worship, the less you worry.

There is nothing that wastes the body like worry, and anyone who has any faith in God should need not to worry about anything whatsoever is to happen in future. Positive thinking is the creation of good imagination. We must first study and after carefully weighing all the facts than only come to a powerful decision. Simply making castles in the air won't solve our problems but add more to our vows. Anxiety and worry can go hand in hand. When anxiety grabs the mind, it is self-perpetuating. Your mind gets clogged with numerous with buts and ifs. Do not worry about your life. Worries are repetitive thoughts associated with feelings of anxiety in anticipation of some negative future event. Yet anxious feelings and the worries that lead to them can prove helpful. It becomes a difficult problem if you are constantly anxious to know as to the happening of the future. It will become a hindrance to your everyday life, rather than motivate you to some good and better things. Worrisome thoughts reproduce faster so one of the most powerful ways to stop the spiral of worry is simply to disclose the worry to a friend. What you eat or drink; or about your body, what you will wear will add to negativity may discard positive thinking.

Happiness comes with Positive Thinking.

If you know that the circumstance is beyond your control or power change than revise it to your liking. Just try to put a stop-less order on your worries. Don't permit little things which become insects of life to ruin your happiness. Co-operate with the inevitable. Decide just how much anxiety a thing may be worth and refuse to give in anymore. All the happiness is not given in one go it comes slowly and slowly with positive thinking. Have worry under your control.

If your worries center around, pay special attention to remain positive and be happy. Keep yourself happy, treat your worried thoughts as valuable signals. How to keep from worrying about criticism?. Simply unjust criticism and think positively and do often discard a bad compliment. It often means that you have aroused jealousy and envy. Let's keep a record of the fool things we have done and stop criticizing ourselves.

Cause of Worry is Negative Thinking- Think Positive

The utmost cause of worry is our negative thinking as it leads us to the state of depression. Worries are there to motivate us and not a mere source of information-gathering and problems. Dejection and Depression is the inability to construct a future. Depression is inertia. That's the thing about depression: But depression is so insidious, and it compounds daily, that it's impossible to ever see the end. Depressed people think they know themselves, but maybe they only know depression. There are no hopeless than this to get depressed. They never even attempt to think positive.

Times will change for the better-Think Positive

Our negative thinking and attitude towards suffering and depression becomes very important because it can affect how we cope with suffering when it arises. Depression is nourished by a lifetime of un-grieved and unforgiven causes. Never worry about your heart till it stops beating. How can you deal with anxiety? You might try what when you did. A person worried so much that he decided to hire someone to do his worrying for him. Times will change for the better when you change. Worry is a misuse of the imagination.

Worry is most often a prideful way of thinking that you have more control over life and its circumstances than you actually do. Positive Thinking leads your way to good and happiness. An art of Good and Happy Living. Neglect worries keep yourself happy, treat your worried thoughts as valuable signals. These are the fundamental facts you should be familiar about worries. A huge factor to stay happy is to cater your worries around, an important relationship in your life and pay special attention sustaining positive relationships. Worries are there to motivate information gathering and problem-solving. Make your mind firm and do come to a positive decision as come what we will not allow the worries to entire our mind and soul. Once a decision is carefully reached we should get busy carrying out our decisions and should not bother about all the anxieties that are about to come. When we, or any of our colleagues or associates, are about to worry about a problem, we must write it out and think positively of the questions: Instead of worrying about what people say of you, why not spend time trying to accomplish something they will admire. What if we just acted like everything was easy? How would your life be different if you stopped worrying about things we can't control and started focusing on the things we can? Let today be the day. You free yourself from fruitless worry, seize the day and take effective action on things you can change. We would change ourselves for the betterment if we start thinking in positive terms. Positive thinking is what is required of us and simply worrying about the future things or as to what will happen in the next moment will certainly deprive us of good and happy living that we are about gather or get in the next hour.

CHAPTER 16

THINK POSITVEAND START HAPPY LIVING

Even when you are facing challenges, it is important to stay open to laughter and humor. Sometimes, simply recognizing the potential humor in a situation can lessen your stress and brighten your outlook. Seeking out sources of humor such as watching a funny sitcom or reading jokes online can help you think more positive thoughts. We need to know and realize that nobody is perfect or flawless. If we try to change the way we look, talk and behave just to please others, and show our pride we will gradually become such a person that we ourselves won't recognize each other and would start and create unnecessary worries within us and our surrounding without being positive and will not start to live happily. We ought to stop worrying over unnecessary things be positive and live without fear happily. As a result, negative thoughts can creep into your mind. While you know that thinking positively is better for your state of mind, you might be surprised to learn that it can also be good for your health. We need to understand that what people think of us is their concern, and not ours. If they think about us to be, too reticent or proud, it's really not our business. If every time we happen to meet some new fellows, we may wonder and imagine as what they think of us, and with this feeling in us we will never be able to live a trouble-free and hassle free life. We are bound to fall into the trap of unnecessary worries denying us the startup of new and the happy living life. We must think rationally. Is it in our hands or can we control what others think about us?. Simply we need to ignore them.

If we cannot, and live our lives the way we want to and find the ways to leave worries aside and start living a happy life. Let us make our way to happy living.

Positive Thinking with Positive Attitudes.

Positive thinking is not about putting on a pair of rose-colored glasses and ignoring all the negative things you will encounter in life. That approach can be just as devastating as ignoring the positive and only focusing on the negative. Balance, with a healthy dose of realism, is the key. It is a well-known fact that attitude decides how a natives or persons copes up with the day to day events of life. Attitude is what a influence a person's reaction to a situation in life is. It sets the emotional undertone for a person to his likes or dislikes a situation even before he is acquainted with it. Positive attitude is a quality that is second to none in a human being. Though we attach so much importance to this attitude, as we grow into teenage and adult years we find ourselves becoming ungrateful or taking things for granted. We lose touch with the very same qualities that we instill in our children. We take for granted our life, our health, our families, the people in our lives, the things that our loved ones do for us to make our lives easier and things that we possess. The attitude of positive speaks a lot about a person. It denotes about changing negative attitudes and making positive thinking a positive attitude a good habit. Thinking positively and a positive attitude help us to appreciate and value ourselves, our potential and all that we have. It ensures that we do not take our abilities for granted. It makes us look at ourselves as special people with a special set of abilities and potential. It banishes the feelings of inadequacy and insecurity that arises from unfair comparisons with others.

It helps us to appreciate people for who they are and not magnify what they are not and their little flaws. It drives away prejudice and makes us approach life with an open mind. It predisposes us to react to the daily events of life in a positive manner and help us to look at the brighter side of life. Make us optimistic. It gives hope and helps us look forward to life with anticipation. We need to know that positive thinking takes the focus away from what we don't have, to appreciating and making good use of what we have. It is closely connected to our emotional wellbeing and happiness. We feel loved and at peace with ourselves for a major part of our lives when we make this attitude ours. This adds and helps us to get rid of greed, amenity, bitterness, jealousy, and promotes a healthy and nurturing attitude towards others, which in turn gets reciprocated and we feel the sense of healthy living We attach so much importance to this attitude of gratitude that when our children fail to thank someone, we insist that they do it. That is what is needed to be avoided from time to time. We expect this in return from others when we help them or give them a gift. We call a person discourteous and rude when they do not say thank us in return.

On the face of it we ought to know that a positive is not an attitude of being satisfied and content, that you never want to do anything, anymore. This is an attitude that makes you feel good about who you are, what you do, and what your potentials are. This attitude impels you to utilize all that you are endowed with as a person, to achieve the highest possible goals. When we have this attitude, we are able to work without any external pressure to perform but there is sufficient pressure and motivation from within. The possessing of positive thinking is like any other habit, so we need to follow the routine of habit formation here as well.

You will win new friends and admirers without having to impress them or conform to the pressure of doing things their way. You will be bubbling with life and the joie de vivre. You will be rearing to go and accomplish all you can with your new found confidence. The best part of adopting the 'positive thinking and a positive attitude of gratitude is that, you will be able to enjoy the smallest pleasures of nature with a heightened sense of satisfaction and awe. I can see and watch a beautiful flower and carry that joy in my mind for future enjoyment with a clear positive habit. I can go back to work freshen and can use it as an object to meditate on when I feel stressed. Let us be clear that a positive is not an attitude of being satisfied and content, that you never want to do anything, anymore. This is an attitude that makes you feel good about who you are, what you do, and what your potentials are. This attitude impels you to utilize all that you are endowed with as a person, to achieve the highest possible goals. When we have this attitude, we are able to work without any external pressure to perform but there is sufficient pressure and motivation from within. The habit of positive thinking is like any other habit, so we need to follow the routine of habit formation here as well.

CHAPTER 17

HAVE POSITVE ATTITUDE

Never let life's hardships disturb you .no one can avoid problems, not even saints or sages. As with any habit, the habit of remaining positive in all situations takes practice and a commitment to yourself to take control. If you tend to think positive you stand to gain all the amenities of a happy life. Positive Thinking leads you to a happy life one must not forgot the life is what you make it, so make it a happy one!. Don't worry on things that may not happen, life is too short to worry too much. Smile and be happy. Make yourself to be positive person. Don't hold onto anything that bothers your mind. It can only hurt your health and it won't help your problems at all. The people that live the longest in this world do not hold grudges or hold or fall prey into negative feelings. Visualize your worries on a large chalkboard in your mind. Watch yourself take a big eraser and erase the problems. Every time the thoughts come back into your head, see yourself with the eraser again. Keep your slate clean and form a habit of thinking positive. We must not worry about tomorrow, for tomorrow will worry about itself. Each day has enough trouble of its own.

Do not anticipate trouble, or worry about what may never happen. Keep in the sunlight. Imagine every day to be a positive day and the last of a life surrounded with hopes,. The hours that come unexpectedly will be much the more grateful. The mind that is anxious about future events is miserable. Present fears are less than horrible imaginings. Positive thinking is sure to ward of every odd imagination and sure to make you a happy person. Positive thinking actually means approaching life's challenges with a positive outlook.

It does not necessarily mean avoiding or ignoring the bad things; instead, it involves making the most of potentially bad situations, trying to see the best in other people, and viewing yourself and your abilities in a positive light. Positive thinking centers on such things as a belief in your abilities, a positive approach to challenges, and trying to make the most of bad situations. Bad things will happen. Sometimes you will be disappointed or hurt by the actions of others. This does not mean that the world is out to get you or that all people will let you down. Instead, positive thinkers will look at the situation realistically, search for ways that they can improve the situation, and try to learn from their experiences. Positive attitude bring good cheer, remembering that the misfortunes hardest to bear are those that never happen, focus on the positive aspects of lives, rather than on the negative setbacks. Let us not waste our lives in doubts and fears. It is not work that kills us, it is worry and the negative thinking. Work is healthy; but worry is rust upon the blade. It is not movement that destroys the machinery, but friction. We need to forget the most disturbing negative thinking in our lives and opt for the positive attitude by following the principles of positive thinking. Not only can positive thinking impact your ability to cope with stress and your immunity, it also has an impact on your overall well-being.

CHAPTER 18

DON'T BE SAD BE HAPPY

Thought which are provoking our mind, about the uncertainties and the negativities, as to what will happen tomorrow. Worries are repetitive thoughts associated with feelings of anxiety in anticipation of some negative future event. Whether the worries are about financial crisis, family problems, work, health or any topic of concern, the anxious feelings produced and sustained by the imaginary thoughts which always distinctly appear to be unpleasant. Worrying will carry tomorrow's load with today's strength. Worry will not empty tomorrow of its sorrows, it empties today of its power and strength. Worries make you to move into tomorrow ahead of time. Half the worry in the world is caused by people trying to make decisions before they have sufficient knowledge on which to base a decision. Why worry about the future. Just imagine as to what if we just acted like everything was easy and there was nothing very serious about it to come in future. Worry often gives a small thing a big shadow and its surrounding do frightened with more scary things. Why worry about tomorrow; concentrate on today happening as for tomorrow will worry about itself. Each day has its own worries and troubles. If there is not any solution to the some problem then do not waste time worrying about it. And if there is a solution to the problem then why waste time worrying about it. Worry will never rob tomorrow of its sorrows, but will only deny today of its meaning happiness and joys.

Worrying is actually a form of superstition and creates false images in our mind and that is the main reason and cause which makes and leads us to this point of imagination. A human being can survive almost anything, as long as he or she sees the end in sight. If something bad or good is to happen it is sure to happen, whether we worry or not. Let us put our energy into today and stop worrying about the future and past. We should not foresee trouble, or worry about what may never happen as past is dead and gone forever and future is uncertain and yet to come. The basic facts we should know about worry. The basic techniques to analyze worry and how to break the worry habit before it breaks us. These are the simple ways where we can concentrate and get rid of worries prevailing in our thoughts. Annalise worry to see and get the reasons and facts of worry. To avoid reoccurrence of worries, concentrate on prayers as prayers are the best source of remedies of the prevailing worries. The more you pray, the less you'll panic.

The more you worship, the less you worry There is nothing that wastes the body like worry, and anyone who has any faith in God should need not to worry about anything whatsoever is to happen in future. We ought to know the basic fundamental of analyzing worries. Worries create unnecessary thoughts and these are caused by people going in for unwanted decisions, fore hand not even knowing as to when a good decision is made and not even having sufficient knowledge about it. We must first study and after carefully weighing all the facts than only come to a powerful decision. Simply making castles in the air won't solve our problems but add more to our vows.

Anxiety and worry can go hand in hand. When anxiety grabs the mind, it is self-perpetuating. Your mind gets clogged with numerous with buts and ifs. Do not worry about your life. Worries are repetitive thoughts associated with feelings of anxiety in anticipation of some negative future event. Yet anxious feelings and the worries that lead to them can prove helpful. It becomes a difficult problem if you are constantly anxious as it will become a hindrance to your everyday life, rather than motivate you to some good and better things. Never worry alone. Worrisome thoughts reproduce faster so one of the most powerful ways to stop the spiral of worry is simply to disclose the worry to a friend. What you will eat or drink; or about your body, what you will wear. If you know that the circumstance is beyond your control or power change than revise it to your liking. Just try to put a stop-less order on your worries. Don't permit little things which become insects of life to ruin your happiness. Co-operate with the inevitable. Decide just how much anxiety a thing may be worth and refuse to give in anymore. All the happiness is not given in one go it comes slowly and slowly.

If your worries center around, an important relationship in your life, pay special attention to remain positive and be happy. To keep yourself happy, treat your worried thoughts as valuable signals. How to keep from worrying about criticism?. Simply unjust criticism is often a disguised compliment. It often means that you have aroused jealousy and envy. Let's keep a record of the fool things we have done and criticize ourselves. The utmost cause of worry is your state of depression. Worries are there to motivate information-gathering and problem-solving.

Depression is the inability to construct a future. Depression is inertia. That's the thing about depression: But depression is so insidious, and it compounds daily, that it's impossible to ever see the end. Depressed people think they know themselves, but maybe they only know depression. There are no hopeless than this to get depressed. Our attitude towards suffering and depression becomes very important because it can affect how we cope with suffering when it arises. Depression is nourished by a lifetime of un grieved and unforgiving causes. Never worry about your heart till it stops beating. How can you deal with anxiety? You might try what when you did. A person worried so much that he decided to hire someone to do his worrying for him. Times will change for the better when you change. Worry is a misuse of the imagination. Worry is most often a prideful way of thinking that you have more control over life and its circumstances than you actually do. To keep yourself happy, treat your worried thoughts as valuable signals. These are the fundamental facts you should be familiar about worries. A huge factor to stay happy is to cater your worries around, an important relationship in your life and pay special attention sustaining positive relationships. Worries are there to motivate information gathering and problem-solving. Make your mind firm and do come to a positive decision as come what we will not allow the worries to entire our mind and soul. Once a decision is carefully reached we should get busy carrying out our decisions and should not bother about all the anxieties that are about to come. When we, or any of our colleagues or associates, are about to worry about a problem, we must write it out and think of the following questions:

Instead of worrying about what people say of you, why not spend time trying to accomplish something they will admire. What if we just acted like everything was easy? How would your life be different if you stopped worrying about things we can't control and started focusing on the things we can?

CHAPTER 19

ENJOY YOUR LIFE

Negative thought which are provoking our mind, about the uncertainties and the negativities, as to what will happen tomorrow creates unnecessary worries and worries are repetitive thoughts associated with feelings of anxiety in anticipation of some negative future event which may end in a failure. Whether the worries are about financial crisis, family problems, work, health or any topic of concern, the anxious feelings and negative thoughts produced are always distinctly unpleasant. Annalise positive thinking and stop worry over petty matters. Worrying will carry tomorrow's load with today's strength. Worry will not empty tomorrow of its sorrows, but it tends to empty today of its power and strength. Worries make you to move into tomorrow ahead of time. Half the worry in the world is caused by people trying to make decisions before they have sufficient knowledge on which to base a decision. Their negative thoughts pressurize them to be away from the positivity in their lives as they fail and do not analysis on positive

Generate Positive Thinking

Why worry about the future. Just imagine as to what if we just acted like everything was easy and there was nothing very serious about it to come in future. Worry often gives a small thing a big shadow and its surrounding do frightened with more scary things.

Why worry about tomorrow; concentrate on today happening as for tomorrow will worry about itself. Each day has its own worries and troubles. Always think positive. If there is not any solution to the some problem then do not waste time worrying about it. And if there is a solution to the problem then why waste time worrying about it. Act fast be positive generate positive thinking worries will automatically vanish in the air. But if you tend to worry they will never rob tomorrow of its sorrows, but will only deny today of its meaning happiness and joys. Negative thoughts only produce worries and worrying is actually a form of superstition and creates false images in our mind and that is the main reason and cause which makes and leads us to this point of imagination. A human being can survive almost anything, as long as he or she sees the end in sight and starts analyzing his positive thoughts. We must not forgot that ff something bad or good is to happen it is sure to happen, whether we worry or not. Let us put our energy into today and stop worrying about the future and past. We should not foresee trouble, or worry about what may never happen as past is dead and gone forever and future is uncertain and yet to come. Positive Thinking will ward off everything and bring happiness in our lives. The basic facts we should know about worry. The basic techniques to analyze worry and how to break the worry habit before it breaks us. These are the simple ways where we can concentrate and get rid of worries prevailing in our thoughts.

Think Positive and Pray- Why Worry?

Annalise positive thinking by annualizing worry you get to see and get the reasons and facts of worry. To avoid reoccurrence of worries, concentrate on prayers as prayers are the best source of remedies of the prevailing worries. Think Positive and Pray. The more you pray, the less you'll panic. The more you worship, the less you worry. There is nothing that wastes the body like worry, and anyone who has any faith in God should need not to worry about anything whatsoever is to happen in future. Positive thinking is the creation of good imagination. We must first study and after carefully weighing all the facts than only come to a powerful decision. Simply making castles in the air won't solve our problems but add more to our vows. Anxiety and worry can go hand in hand. When anxiety grabs the mind, it is self-perpetuating. Your mind gets clogged with numerous with buts and ifs. Do not worry about your life. Worries are repetitive thoughts associated with feelings of anxiety in anticipation of some negative future event. Yet anxious feelings and the worries that lead to them can prove helpful. It becomes a difficult problem if you are constantly anxious to know as to the happening of the future. It will become a hindrance to your everyday life, rather than motivate you to some good and better things. Worrisome thoughts reproduce faster so one of the most powerful ways to stop the spiral of worry is simply to disclose the worry to a friend. What you eat or drink; or about your body, what you will wear will add to negativity may discard positive thinking.

Happiness comes with Positive Thinking.

If you know that the circumstance is beyond your control or power change than revise it to your liking. Just try to put a stop-less order on your worries. Don't permit little things which become insects of life to ruin your happiness. Co-operate with the inevitable. Decide just how much anxiety a thing may be worth and refuse to give in anymore. All the happiness is not given in one go it comes slowly and slowly with positive thinking. Have worry under your control. If your worries center around, pay special attention to remain positive and be happy. Keep yourself happy, treat your worried thoughts as valuable signals. How to keep from worrying about criticism?. Simply unjust criticism and think positively and do often discard a bad compliment. It often means that you have aroused jealousy and envy. Let's keep a record of the fool things we have done and stop criticizing ourselves.

Cause of Worry is Negative Thinking- Think Positive

The utmost cause of worry is our negative thinking as it leads us to the state of depression. Worries are there to motivate us and not a mere source of information-gathering and problems. Dejection and Depression is the inability to construct a future. Depression is inertia. That's the thing about depression: But depression is so insidious, and it compounds daily, that it's impossible to ever see the end. Depressed people think they know themselves, but maybe they only know depression. There are no hopeless than this to get depressed. They never even attempt to think positive.

Times will change for the better-Think Positive

Our negative thinking and attitude towards suffering and depression becomes very important because it can affect how we cope with suffering when it arises. Depression is nourished by a lifetime of un-grieved and unforgiven causes. Never worry about your heart till it stops beating. How can you deal with anxiety? You might try what when you did. A person worried so much that he decided to hire someone to do his worrying for him. Times will change for the better when you change. Worry is a misuse of the imagination. Worry is most often a prideful way of thinking that you have more control over life and its circumstances than you actually do. Positive Thinking leads your way to good and happiness. An art of Good and Happy Living. Neglect worries keep yourself happy, treat your worried thoughts as valuable signals. These are the fundamental facts you should be familiar about worries. A huge factor to stay happy is to cater your worries around, an important relationship in your life and pay special attention sustaining positive relationships. Worries are there to motivate information gathering and problem-solving. Make your mind firm and do come to a positive decision as come what we will not allow the worries to entire our mind and soul.

Once a decision is carefully reached we should get busy carrying out our decisions and should not bother about all the anxieties that are about to come. When we, or any of our colleagues or associates, are about to worry about a problem, we must write it out and think positively of the questions: Instead of worrying about what people say of you, why not spend time trying to accomplish something they will admire. What if we just acted like everything was easy?

How would your life be different if you stopped worrying about things we can't control and started focusing on the things we can? Let today be the day. You free yourself from fruitless worry, seize the day and take effective action on things you can change. We would change ourselves for the betterment if we start thinking in positive terms. Positive thinking is what is required of us and simply worrying about the future things or as to what will happen in the next moment will certainly deprive us of good and happy living that we are about gather or get in the next hour.

CHAPTER 20

GENERATE HAPPINESS IN YOU

If you are interested in getting more happiness, focus on all the ways as if you have already attained success. You need to focus on the thing and create a live within you. If you want love and affection, focus on all the people and the abundance of love that you have to give to them. If we want to have greater health, focus on all the ways that we are healthy, thus creating and delivering a good life within you. You need to admit that there are problems that you cannot change. But you can change the way of your thinking if you identify the main reason of the problem. And if you acknowledge the facts, that you have been negative or inactive in finding a solution to the problem, probably this will make it easier for you to become positive thus creating a new lease of life within you. You must try to make goals. Making goals can give you a more positive outlook on life. People often tend to get bored with life and get the feeling that they are stuck to negative things which the result they often get the feeling of being depressed. Setting a direction for yourself and a goal would surely help you to move forward. If you expecting to succeed, and are not afraid of failure, you have the best chance of staying positive and can create a very positive life within you. When you, or any of your associates, are tempted to worry about a problem, write out the solution and a definite answer to it. This helps a positive feeling to generate within you.

Another thing you need to understand is that there are several ways to cultivate a mental attitude that can bring you peace and happiness and can carnage a good life within you. More of it if you fill your mind with thoughts of peace, courage, health, and hope, your life will be easy to live. You would get a happy feeling of life and mind. If you let yourself to forget your own unhappiness, by trying to create a little happiness for others. You are best to yourself. The perfect way to conquer worry is the Prayer of God. To keep yourself from worrying about criticism, do not even try to get mixed with your enemies, because if you do you will hurt yourself far more than we hurting them. Instead of worrying about ingratitude, let's expect it. Let's remember that the only way to find happiness is not to expect gratitude, but to give for the joy of giving. Let us build a happy life within us….generate peace and a healthy atmosphere around us. This will help us to lead a peaceful happy and prosperous life and we would find ourselves to be happier than before. You should do things in the order of their importance.

You need to clear your desk of all papers except those relating to the immediate problem at hand. When you face a problem, solve it then and there, if you have the facts to make a decision. Make a decision fast and do not linger on. Learn to organize, deputize, and supervise and straight away come to decision. Simply postponing it would spoil your good thoughts and there is every likelihood your mind may get into negative activities and start thinking in negative manner. Therefore write down a list of things that make you excited, however big, small, likely or unlikely. Then work to make them occur more often.

Look for moments of joy and savor them. Recognize your good happening every day. Eat well do plenty of exercise and do not skip meals It is a known fact that Physical exercise is known to stimulate our veins and get to strengthen our minds that lift depression and anxiety so we need to walk, swim, run or whatever we like doing best. Those who create or those who do well on the worst scenario, give themselves worry and stress, tend to be devastated. If we cannot get some sunshine, we can always lighten up our rooms with brighter lights. We can have lunch outside the office. Take frequent walks instead of driving our cars over short distances. No man is indispensable. First of all our circle of friends is always there to give us some moral support. Spending time and engaging ourselves in worthwhile activities could give us a very enjoyable and satisfying feeling. Nothing feels better than having group support. Good friends are quite important and their company generally lightened up our spirits. T

o get to know and to find such friends we simply have to be friendly with ourselves, and then the friendships will naturally follow us. We need to understand the power of touch and support and we have not to underestimate it strength and support. Don't we feel so good when someone pats us on our back and gives us some words of encouragement during your most challenging times and difficult times? Just hug or embrace someone someday you will see that you have almost changed his life. Get intimate with him and try to establish close ties with his family and friends.

The love and care expressed by you will tremendously boost him and well as your immune system and fury of worry will be diminished for all. In our lives storms may come and go in the form of reversals, but if we have the power and foundation of inner fulfillment and if we deal with it with a very clear practical mind these storms will not kill us or will not disrupt us. There could be numberless reasons for which we keep on worrying. We may be worried about our health, wealth, loved ones, friends, the happening f yesterday and the follow happenings of tomorrow, the environment or the world politics, but these can be dealt with firm mind and fearless worry if we generate within ourselves the power of enlightenment within ourselves.

CHAPTER 21

STEPS FOR HAPPY LIFE

The secret of successful and happy life lies in keeping ourselves smiling and the character which is the foremost important reason that lies within us. Do not be curious about anything, but in everything, by prayer and petition, with thanksgiving, present your requests to God. Whenever your mind is tempted to jump the fence and start to worry, say this verse aloud or to yourself. You may even have to repeat it over and over again. Am I constantly striving to see the positive in every aspect of my life?. Steps for a successful and happy life. At time we may think that there is no road is left for us from where we can achieve the happiness of our lives. We may also feel that life has become terrible for us to live and we are carrying new hope that someone would come to rescue us. There may be chances that someone who was there with us before might have held on to us when we were on the dark side of the life. We should not forget that happiness in life comes through the doors of positive thoughts; we need to have them first. If one door happen to close, another opens, in the event only when we are confident and optimistic. We have so many reasons to cry and at the same time plenty of reasons to smile as well. Similarly, happiness does not stand for anything, but is on our way of thinking that how do we keep ourselves happy in life. Failure and disappointment are part of our life. The only thing is that we need to face and solve the problem is by keeping our dreams and hope alive be it a reason that success and happiness will come our way again. The experience has taught us that we should buy some strength, hope and positivity from our loved ones to help ourselves in such a situation rather than surrendering as life is a precious gift of

God and is equipped with full of joy and happiness if we help ourselves in these critical moments we can live with considerable optimism. What if when everything goes wrong and all the doors of happiness are closed our live becomes a silent. It is a quite common and we are aware of a marvelous proverb that Life itself is a stage and we all are the performers, performing different acts assigned to us by our almighty power. We should not forget as to what is in our possession? if it is to fulfill our duties towards our responsibility and do whatever is correct and is allowed by us in our life?. However, despite of all these good thoughts which are embodied to us by the almighty fail to revive these unwanted circumstances that lead us to sorrow and difficulties and a situation where we do not know what is correct and good for us and what is wrong for us.We should always remember that, "Life is there, where there is hope". That single thing that remains in our hands is to find out ways to know how to overcome these worries of our life at that very moment when all doors are closed for us which means that whatever situation is there, we must not give up hope. We must fight because there have been always a chance that with good faith and hard work we can turn the odds in our favor. It is often said that it is very easy to advise but when it comes to us, things go out of our control and we fail to suggest a way out for ourselves. We fall into the trap of unnecessary worries and elope ourselves with negative thoughts. We feel better when somebody else is facing some difficulty but when it comes to us we fail to gather that faith, will power and the words of strength. It is a common fact that no one in this world is free of obstacles or difficulties. If all the openings of happiness are shut for us and we have to overcome that and have no way to come out, but to survive lest we must have to learn to swim out of the sorrows because this is what is called life and sorrow free living.

There are lot more examples and in many other situations, where we will find that how we could have faced and fought with our sorrows and difficulties of life when there was no hope left in our lives. When the power of will is at the worst and each one of us knows that the one who is gone never comes back. Neither a thousands of words would not be enough to bring him back nor a million tears, because each and every moment, eyes would only shed tears , mind would remain tensed and we would be simply surrounded by worries and the life seems to have been vanished. Life is ever expanding, contraction is death. As commonly said by big saints that the self- seeking man who is looking after his personal comforts and leading a lazy life for himself there would be no room for him even in the hell and he simply have lost the power of his will.We are quite aware of the fact that faith in oneself is the history of a man and that faith calls the quality of superiority within a person. One cannot do anything without it. We fail only when we do not try very hard to achieve the power and faith within us. As soon as we lose faith, death comes in our way and we are surrounds by all the evils and stupid worries of the world. The secret and history of every successful man is to have, good confidence, faith and strength behind him and that remain the right cause of his single success in life. Unselfishness plays a very vital role in his life. He may not have been perfectly unselfish, yet he was tending towards it. If he had been perfectly unselfish, he would have been as great a success. The degree of unselfishness marks the degree of success everywhere and he leads to be successful man without fear worries and selfishness. There are quite a number of reasons to believe that for a successful and happy life the mystery surrounding it lies in our interests, and good memory which is the basis of our interest, power of desire and aim, keeping ourselves smiling and the doubt free character which is the foremost important reason for a successful and happy life.

If we possess one solid unselfish and doubt free character within ourselves we would be quite happy and successful. The love for God and worshipping God adds to one common thing the immense faith in Him. There may be different beliefs and ways to worship God in different communities, places and religions, but one thing remains the same and that is the Love of God for all of us. Our world is full of odds and evens, happiness and sorrows, fulfilment and emptiness. And these are all created by the Almighty. However, the most beautiful Gift of God, is Human, which is such a mystery driven by Him which could hardly be defined or explained in depth. We know that life cannot be foreseen. Life is not a bed of roses. Life is a battle field and not a bed of roses as every man on earth has to struggle very hard in making his life happy. If aim of our life is to stay happy and let others to be happy, we will be happy and remembered by all. But no one will actually remember us for the wealth we have gained, or success we have achieved. I have no aim in life. Summary living with no purpose in life is just like a feather moving towards the wind. Both career and purpose are different issues but it is equally important to understand the value of these things which would ultimately add spicy flavor to your living. Innovation at work place is what is it necessary how well we judge our work, how good we like and enjoy it. If we take our work as a stiff challenge and as learning every day, then we would start loving it and giving our best. However, if we just work for the sake of then nothing is realized and we do not remain happy in life. Life is such a special gift of Almighty and it is not gifted by Him to use it the way we like or love to. The actual path shown by Him needs to be followed by us for us to reach the peak of betterment every moment. We need to have some positive attitude to look at it comfortably but at the same time having a positive mental attitude does not mean banishing all negative thoughts and people from your life.

The same is true with thoughts. When we go to field with negative thoughts, we banish one and another one arises. Therefore creation of positivity in life is utmost necessary to enjoy the special gift of God to us. Now let's us imagine that we are not feeling at our best today, and we are having thoughts that could be classified as negative. We shouldn't be thinking such negative thoughts. We don't like the negative thoughts. We ought to know that negative thoughts are stressful, demoralizing and depressing. We shouldn't aim to have negative thoughts at all. Often we feel uncomfortable because we think we have to say or do something in response to another person's words. When we find ourselves thinking this way, it helps enormously to take a few moments to check inside and notice what we are feeling. We are deeply depressed that negativity has governed us and has taken a deep root in our minds If we want to live a positive, joyful life, we must not be surrounded by negative people who don't encourage our happiness. As a negative person, we ought to get attracted too negative people only. Only when we decide to make the change to live a more positive life, we have to get rid of our lives of the most negative influences in it. We are quite aware of the fact that no one is perfect and perfection isn't the goal when it comes to positivity but there were people in our lives who were consistently negative, who constantly bring us down, we need to stop spending so much time with them. We can very well imagine; it is not easy for us to get away from these negative people. It can hurt us to keep distance from people even when you know they aren't good for us and for our current lifestyle. In addition to removing negative influences from them, we also have to get rid of some of our own negative behaviors, such as the drug and alcohol abuse. We need to take some concrete steps and examine which behaviors are good for us and which were not harmful.

What we need is to learn to focus on the positive things, such as working on positive activities and cultivating new, positive relationships. We must let go of the negative ones. This process may be not easy to live a positive life when negative people and behaviors continually pull us down.In every situation or in every person there is something good. Most of the time it's not easy to find the positive qualities but we have to look hard to discover positivity in them. Now, when we are faced with a difficult or challenging situation, we need to think and talk to ourselves and console our mind, no matter how terrible the situation might seem, we can always find something good if we take the time to think about it. It is quite obvious that anything good and bad is learning experience so, at the very least, we must learn from bad experiences. However, there's usually even more to it than that. If you really take some time to have a look at it, we would find something good, something genuinely positive, about every person or situation.

Once we start thinking more positively, we will realize that we had to reinforce these thoughts and behaviors within ourselves so that we could stick to it. As with any sort of training, the more we practice, the better we get to be positive. The best and easiest way to do this is to be positive when it comes to who we are.

We need to speak to ourselves that we are awesome. And we have done a good job at work thus creating positivity within us. We need to be honest with ourselves, and we need to do our best to look for the good. And, whatever we do, we must not focus on the negative. It is alright not to like everything about ourselves, but don't focus on what we don't like. We have all the positive attributes, and it's up to us to remind ourselves of them every day.

Not only do we need to be positive with ourselves for this multiple action to take effect, but we need to be more positive with others. We have to share our wealth of positivity with the people of the world. The best way is to be nice with other people, no matter what. Tell them that they look nice today. Appreciate their job and tell them that have done a great job on that assignment. Be positive and tell your elder or your kids how much you love them and how great they are. When someone is feeling down, do what we need to do is to cheer him or her up. Do send them gifts nice flower and glow them with nice notes.

CHAPTER 22

CREATE HAPPINESS AND GOOD LIVING

If you are interested in getting more happiness, focus on all the ways as if you have already attained success. You need to focus on the thing and create a live within you. Positive thinking will generate happiness in you. Our actions positive thinking breed confidence and courage in us. If we want to conquer fear, anger and worry we should sit ideal and just think about it. Let our deep worrying do some advance thinking and planning. If we look into our own mind and heart, and we will find nothing wrong there, what is there to worry about and generate unhappiness in us?

Is there anything to be unhappy about?

Practically nothing what is there to be unhappy about? So why worry unnecessarily and make our present and future dark. Discard negative thought think positive and be happy. Positive thinking is the key to all problems and worries. Solve all your problems and get rid of all unnecessary worries by simply thinking in a positive manner. What is there to worry about? Think positive, be positive and have confidence in you. You will create great happiness within yourself. You need to admit that there are problems that you cannot change. But you can change the way of your thinking if you identify the main reason of the problem. And if you acknowledge the facts, that you have been negative or inactive in finding a solution to the problem, probably this will make it easier for you to become positive thus creating a new lease of life within you.

You must try to make goals.

Making goals can give you a more positive outlook on life. People often tend to get bored with life and get the feeling that they are stuck to negative things which the result they often get the feeling of being depressed. Setting a direction for yourself and a goal would surely help you to move forward. If you expecting to succeed, and are not afraid of failure, you have the best chance of staying positive and can create a very positive life within you. When you, or any of your associates, are tempted to worry about a problem, write out the solution and a definite answer to it. This helps a positive feeling to generate within you.

There are several ways to cultivate a mental attitude.

Another thing you need to understand is that there are several ways to cultivate a mental attitude that can bring you peace and happiness and can carnage a good life within you. More of it if you fill your mind with thoughts of peace, courage, health, and hope, your life will be easy to live. You would get a happy feeling of life and mind if you let yourself to forget your own unhappiness, by trying to create a little happiness for others. You are best to yourself. The perfect way to conquer worry is the Prayer of God. To keep yourself from worrying about criticism, do not even try to get mixed with your enemies, because if you do you will hurt yourself far more than we hurting them. Instead of worrying about ingratitude, let's expect it. Let's remember that the only way to find happiness is not to expect gratitude, but to give for the joy of giving. Let us build a happy life within us generate peace and a healthy atmosphere around us.

Let us build a happy life within us

This will help us to lead a peaceful happy and prosperous life and we would find ourselves to be happier than before. You should do things in the order of their importance. You need to clear your desk of all papers except those relating to the immediate problem at hand. When you face a problem, solve it then and there, if you have the facts to make a decision. Make a decision fast and do not linger on.to earn to organize, deputize, and supervise and straight away come to decision. Simply postponing it would spoil your good thoughts and there is every likelihood your mind may get into negative activities and start thinking in negative manner. Therefore write down a list of things that make you excited, however big, small, likely or unlikely. Then work to make them occur more often. Look for moments of joy and savor them. Recognize your good happening every day.

Eat well do plenty of exercise and do not skip meals.

It is a known fact that physical exercise is known to stimulate our veins and get to strengthen our minds that lift depression and anxiety so we need to walk, swim, run or whatever we like doing best. Those who create or those who do well on the worst scenario, give themselves worry and stress, tend to be devastated. If we cannot get some sunshine, we can always lighten up our rooms with brighter lights. We can have lunch outside the office. Take frequent walks instead of driving our cars over short distances. No man is indispensable. First of all our circle of friends is always there to give us some moral support.

Spending time and engaging ourselves in worthwhile activities could give us a very enjoyable and satisfying feeling. Nothing feels better than having group support. Good friends are quite important and their company generally lightened up our spirits. To get to know and to find such friends we simply have to be friendly with ourselves, and then the friendships will naturally follow us. We need to understand the power of touch and support and we have not to underestimate it strength and support. Don't we feel so good when someone pats us on our back and gives us some words of encouragement during your most challenging times and difficult times? Just hug or embrace someone someday you will see that you have almost changed his life. Get intimate with him and try to establish close ties with his family and friends. The love and care expressed by you will tremendously boost him and well as your immune system and fury of worry will be diminished for all.

In our lives storms may come and go.

In our lives storms may come and go. in the form of reversals, but if we have the power and foundation of inner fulfillment and if we deal with it with a very clear practical mind these storms will not kill us or will not disrupt us. There could be numberless reasons for which we keep on worrying. We may be worried about our health, wealth, loved ones, friends, the happening of yesterday and the follow happenings of tomorrow, the environment or the world politics, but these can be dealt with firm mind and fearless worry if we generate within ourselves the power of enlightenment within ourselves.

There's no sense in worrying about the negatives if these negatives cannot be changed. If we waste energy and happiness on the things we can't change, we'll only make ourselves more frustrated and come to the stage of depression dejection and disappointments.

Negativity is a habit.

Negativity is a habit and we often don't realize we're doing ourselves down. Under each negative thought that we have written, we can spot an alternative way of looking at it, that isn't so negative. Take your mind to positivity and mold and drive your thoughts to the positivity. There's a world of difference between expecting failure or rejection so as not to be disappointed when it occurs and recognizing it as a possibility of being positive. It's sensible to look at a situation from all angles and to have a back-up plan to fall back on if need be. People who do this will not see failure as another step on the road to eventual success; but by expecting and envisioning success, there's less likely to be a failure. Let us find some ways of removing negative thoughts and discouraging our worries to be born.

Let us all generate and create happiness within us

Let us all generate and create happiness within us by removing all negative thoughts negative feeling and unwanted desires that make our mind greedy and spoil the charm of our sweet good and happy living.

CHAPTER 23

CREATE GOOD AND HAPPY LIFE

It might not be easy, but the positive impact it will have on our mental, emotional, and physical health will be well-worth it .At time we may think that there is no road is left for us from where we can achieve the happiness of our lives. We may also feel that life has become terrible for us to live and we are carrying new hope that someone would come to rescue us. There may be chances that someone who was there with us before might have held on to us when we were on the dark side of the life.

Life itself is a stage and we all are the performers.

What if when everything goes wrong and all the doors of happiness are closed our live becomes a silent. It is a quite common and we are aware of a marvelous proverb that Life itself is a stage and we all are the performers, performing different acts assigned to us by our almighty power. We should not forget as to what is in our possession, if it is to fulfill our duties towards our responsibility and do whatever is correct and is allowed by us in our life? We should not forget that happiness in life comes through the doors of positive thoughts; we need to have them first. If one door happen to close, another opens, in the event only when we are confident and optimistic. We have so many reasons to cry and at the same time plenty of reasons to smile as well. Similarly, happiness does not stand for anything, but is on our way of thinking that how do we keep ourselves happy in life. Failure and disappointment are part of our life.

The only thing is that we need to face and solve the problem is by keeping our dreams and hope alive be it a reason that success and happiness will come our way again.

Smiling and the doubt free character which is the foremost important reason for a successful and happy life.

There are quite a number of reasons to believe that for a successful and happy life the mystery surrounding it lies in our interests, and good memory which is the basis of our interest, power of desire and aim, keeping ourselves smiling and the doubt free character which is the foremost important reason for a successful and happy life. If we possess one solid unselfish and doubt free character within ourselves we would be quite happy and successful. The experience has taught us that we should buy some strength, hope and positivity from our loved ones to help ourselves in such a situation rather than surrendering as life is a precious gift of God and is equipped with full of joy and happiness if we help ourselves in these critical moments we can live with considerable optimism. Now let's us imagine that we are not feeling at our best today, and we are having thoughts that could be classified as negative.

We shouldn't be thinking such negative thoughts. We don't like the negative thoughts. We ought to know that negative thoughts are stressful, demoralizing and depressing. We shouldn't aim to have negative thoughts at all. Often we feel uncomfortable because we think we have to say or do something in response to another person's words.

When we find ourselves thinking this way, it helps enormously to take a few moments to check inside and notice what we are feeling. We are deeply depressed that negativity has governed us and has taken a deep root in our minds. So, let's imagine that you have chosen to focus on your negative thinking with regards to school.

Evaluating thoughts can generate happiness within us.

The next step is to spend a little bit of time each day evaluating your own thoughts. When you find yourself thinking critical thoughts about yourself, take a moment to pause and reflect. While you might be upset about getting a bad grade on an exam, is berating yourself really the best approach? Is there any way to put a positive spin on the situation? While you might not have done well on this exam, at least you have a better indication of how to structure your study time for the next big test. However, despite of all these good thoughts which are embodied to us by the almighty fail to revive these unwanted circumstances that lead us to sorrow and difficulties and a situation where we do not know what is correct and good for us and what is wrong for us.

Life is there, where there is hope.

We should always remember that, "Life is there, where there is hope". That single thing that remains in our hands is to find out ways to know how to overcome these worries of our life at that very moment when all doors are closed for us which means that whatever situation is there, we must not give up hope.

We must fight because there have been always a chance that with good faith and hard work we can turn the odds in our favor. It is often said that it is very easy to advice but when it comes to us, things go out of our control and we fail to suggest a way out for ourselves.

Happy living allows us to tackle life's challenges

We fall into the trap of unnecessary worries and elope ourselves with negative thoughts. We feel better when somebody else is facing some difficulty but when it comes to us we fail to gather that faith, will power and the words of strength. Being a positive thinker is not about ignoring reality in favor of aspirational thoughts. It is more about taking a proactive approach to our lives. Instead of feeling hopeless or overwhelmed, positive thinking allows us to tackle life's challenges by looking for effective ways to resolve conflict and come up with creative solutions to problems. It might not be easy, but the positive impact it will have on our mental, emotional, and physical health will be well-worth it. It takes practice; lots of practice. This is not a step-by-step process that we can complete and be done with. Instead, it involves a lifelong commitment to looking inside ourselves and being willing to challenge negative thoughts and make positive changes. It is a common fact that no one in this world is free of obstacles or difficulties. If all the openings of happiness are shut for us and we have to overcome that and have no way to come out, but to survive lest we must have to learn to swim out of the sorrows because this is what is called life and sorrow free living.

There are lot more examples and in many other situations, where we will find that how we could have faced and fought with our sorrows and difficulties of life when there was no hope left in our lives. As commonly said by big saints that the self- seeking man who is looking after his personal comforts and leading a lazy life for himself there would be no room for him even in the hell and he simply have lost the power of his will and he cannot lead a happy life.

The secret of every successful man is to have, good confidence

The secret of every successful man is to have, good confidence, faith and strength behind him and that remain the right cause of his single success in life. Unselfishness plays a very vital role in his life. He may not have been perfectly unselfish, yet he was tending towards it. If he had been perfectly unselfish, he would have been as great a success. The degree of unselfishness marks the degree of success everywhere and he leads to be successful man without fear worries and selfishness. Therefore creation of positivity in life is utmost necessary to enjoy the special gift of God to us. The love for God and worshipping God adds to one common thing the immense faith in Him. There may be different beliefs and ways to worship God in different communities, places and religions, but one thing remains the same and that is the Love of God for all of us. Our world is full of odds and evens, happiness and sorrows, fulfilment and emptiness. And these are all created by the Almighty.

However, the most beautiful Gift of God, is Human, which is such a mystery driven by Him which could hardly be defined or explained in depth.

If aim of our life is to stay happy and let others to be happy, we will be happy and remembered by all.

We know that life cannot be foreseen. Life is not a bed of roses. Life is a battle field and not a bed of roses as every man on earth has to struggle very hard in making his life happy. But no one will actually remember us for the wealth we have gained, or success we have achieved until and unless we do not live a happy life. Life is such a special gift of Almighty and it is not gifted by Him to use it the way we like or love to. The actual path shown by Him needs to be followed by us for us to reach the peak of betterment every moment. We need to have some positive attitude to look at it comfortably but at the same time having a positive mental attitude does not mean banishing all negative thoughts and people from your life. We need to believe that a positive attitude is a choice. This step is hard to take. People are either positive or negative. They tend to blame their negativity on all kinds of outside forces fate, experiences, parents, relationship, but never really stopped to think that they could choose to be positive. Piercing ourselves that positivity is a choice has been one of the greatest things we have ever done for ourselves. Now when we find ourselves in a bad situation, we know that it's up to us to find the good, to be positive regardless of what's happening around us. We should no longer point fingers and place blame to anyone else.

We need to realize that everything happens how it happens, and it's up to us to choose how we want to feel about it. We need to be in control of our attitude, and no one can take that away this from us. If we want to live a positive, joyful and happy life, we must not be surrounded by negative people who don't encourage our happiness. As a negative person, we ought to get attracted too negative people only. Only when we decide to make the change to live a more positive life, we have to get rid of our lives of the most negative influences in it. We are quite aware of the fact that no one is perfect and perfection isn't the goal when it comes to positivity but there were people in our lives who were consistently negative, who constantly bring us down, we need to stop spending so much time with them.

We can very well imagine, it is not easy for us to get away from these negative people.

It can hurt us to keep distance from people even when you know they aren't good for us and for our current lifestyle. In addition to removing negative influences from them, we also have to get rid of some of our own negative behaviors, such as the drug and alcohol abuse. We need to take some concrete steps and examine which behaviors are good for us and which were not harmful. What we need is to learn to focus on the positive things, such as working on positive activities and cultivating new, positive relationships. We must let go of the negative ones. This process may be not easy to live a positive life when negative people and behaviors continually pull us down. In every situation or in every person there is something good.

Anything good and bad is learning experience.

Most of the time it's not easy to find the positive qualities but we have to look hard to discover positivity in them. Now, when we are faced with a difficult or challenging situation, we need to think and talk to ourselves and console our mind, no matter how terrible the situation might seem, we can always find something good if we take the time to think about it. It is quite obvious that anything good and bad is learning experience so, at the very least, we must learn from bad experiences. However, there's usually even more to it than that. If you really take some time to have a look at it, we would find something good, something genuinely positive, about every person or situation. Not only do we need to be happy with ourselves for this multiple action to take effect, but we also need to be more positive and happy with others. We have to share our wealth of happiness with the people of the world. The best way is to be nice with other people, no matter what. Tell them that they look nice today. Appreciate their job and tell them that have done a great job on that assignment. Be happy and tell your elder or your kids how much you love them and how great they are.

When someone is feeling down, do what we need to do is to cheer him or her up. Do send them gifts nice flower and glow them with nice notes. By doing this we will not make ourselves happy but in turn give and generate happiness for others too. At times we may suffer from chronic depression, though we know how good things look on to others life cannot be worse for us. Let's imagine how to deal when life leaves a great big steaming pile at our doorstep.

Lest we need to remember that external factors can be dealt with by taking positive and happy steps to repair or at least address the root of the problem as best as we can. Whatever may be the primary cause of the problem, that cause must be examined first? What is required is that we never wanted to see the good in ourselves and, therefore, didn't want to see it in others also. We must not be critical and condescending rather we must be encouraging and supportive. We should not try to treat others as we would like to be treated, but also try to consider how we would like to be treated. The world likes to appreciate positivity, and the more we share it with others, the more we would be practicing it your own lives. When we start feeling like the idea of not being a happy person we need to remind ourselves that all it takes is one tiny step in the right direction to move towards a more happy life.

Share your happy thoughts with others

We have to believe in ourselves and remember the most important lesson of all is a happy outlook and that is a choice that we can always make. The power of remaining happy, whatever the situation, can never be underestimated. We are all here for a short duration, but is it worth it to spend any of that time in a any angry or being negative? That need to sort out in mind and soul and thus must share our happy thoughts with others. The real test of any one is to remain happy whenever some challenges become difficult. Remaining happy keeps our mind in the right state of balance and often opens resolutions to the problems at hand.

Negativity is contagious and spreads like fire. It not only does its affect anyone, but it spreads to everyone who ever comes in contact with it or whoever they interact with. When only the negative perspective is in focus, the resolution process is impeded. Eliminating negativity, or rather, being positive is a mindset that can be found at any moment, and which can be turned into a habit. We must throw away the negativity in us and opt for being a very positive person this in turn will make us happy and we would be able to lead a sweet and happy life forever.

CHAPTER 24

MAKE YOUR WAY TO HAPPY LIVING

We need to learn a lesson from every situation. No matter how difficult the situation may appear. We should recognize the beautiful lessons waiting to be discovered. Sometimes lessons may prove to be expensive and costly, but every problem is a learning experience in disguise. We need to be conscious of our thoughts, especially, when life just isn't going our way. The moment we see that we are diving into frustration, agony, sorrow or low self –esteem we must shift our thoughts, by thinking about something completely different and unrelated. You are essentially trying to cultivate a new habit here, the secret of successful and happy life lies in keeping ourselves smiling and the character which is the foremost important reason that lies within us. Whenever your mind is tempted to jump the fence and start to worry, say this verse aloud or to yourself. You may even have to repeat it over and over again. Am I constantly striving to see the positive in every aspect of my life? Steps for a successful and happy life.

MAKE YOUR WAY TO HAPPY LIVING

We need to believe that a happy living is a matter of our choice. This step is hard to take. People are either positive or negative. They tend to blame their negativity on all kinds of outside forces fate, experiences, parents, relationship, but never really stopped to think that they could choose to be happy. Piercing ourselves that happiness is a choice has been one of the greatest things we have ever done for ourselves.

Now when we find ourselves in a bad situation, we know that it is up to us to find the good, to be happy regardless of what is happening around us. We should no longer point fingers and place blame to anyone else. We need to realize that everything happens how it happens, and it is up to us to choose how we want to feel about it. We need to be in control of our attitude and happiness, and no one can take that away this from us.

Unhappiness is contagious and spreads like fire.

It not only does its affect anyone, but it spreads to everyone who ever comes in contact with it or whoever they interact with. When only the negative perspective is in focus, the resolution process is impeded. Eliminating unhappiness, or rather, being happy is a mindset that can be found at any moment, and which can be turned into a habit. If we want to live a happy, joyful life, we must not be surrounded by negative people who don't encourage our happiness. As a negative person, we ought to get attracted to negative people only. Only when we decide to make the change to live a more positive and happy life, we have to get rid of our lives of the most negative influences in it.

We are quite aware of the fact that no one is perfect and perfection is not the goal when it comes to positivity but there were people in our lives who were consistently negative, who constantly bring us down, we need to stop spending so much time with them. We can very well imagine, it is not easy for us to get away from these unhappy people. It can hurt us to keep distance from people even when you know they are not good for us and for our current lifestyle.

In addition to removing negative influences from them, we also have to get rid of some of our own negative behaviors, such as the drug and alcohol abuse. We need to take some concrete steps and examine which behaviors are good for us and which were not harmful. What we need is to learn to focus on the happy things, such as working on positive activities and cultivating new, positive relationships. We must let go of the negative ones. This process may be not easy to live a positive life when negative people and behaviors continually pull us down. We need to discard all of them to lead a happy and sweet life. An art of sweet living lies below us we have only to recognize it.

Look For Sweet Living in Life

The real test of any one is to remain happy whenever some challenges become difficult. Remaining happy keeps our mind in the right state of balance and often opens resolutions to the problems at hand. We must throw away the unhappiness in us and opt for being a very positive person. In every situation or in every person there is something good. Most of the time it's not easy to find the happiness qualities but we have to look hard to discover happiness in them. Now, when we are faced with a difficult or challenging situation, we need to think and talk to ourselves and console our mind, no matter how terrible the situation might seem, we can always find something good if we take the time to think about it. It is quite obvious that anything good and bad is learning experience so, at the very least, we must learn from bad experiences. However, there is usually even more to it than that.

If you really take some time to have a look at it, we would find something good, something genuinely happy, about every person or situation. We must look for sweet living in life

Get Sweet feeling in your life

Once we start thinking more in a happy manner, we will realize that we had to reinforce these thoughts and behaviors within ourselves so that we could stick to it. As with any sort of training, the more we practice, the better we get to be happy. The best and easiest way to do this is to be happy when it comes to who we are. We need to speak to ourselves that we are awesome. And we have done a good job at work thus creating happiness within us. We need to be honest with ourselves, and we need to do our best to look for the good. And, whatever we do, we must not focus on the negative. It is alright not to like everything about ourselves, but don not focus on what we do not like. We have all to get the sweet feeling in our lives, and it is up to us to remind ourselves of them every day.

Share sweet and happy thoughts

Not only do we need to be happy with ourselves for this multiple action to take effect, but we need to be more happy with others too. We have to share our wealth of happiness with the people of the world. The best way is to be nice with other people and to make them happy, no matter what the matter is. Tell them that they look nice today. What is required is that we never wanted to see the good in ourselves and, therefore, didn't want to see it in others also.

We must not be critical and condescending rather we must be encouraging and supportive. We should not try to treat others as we would like to be treated, but also try to consider how we would like to be treated. This will strangle the pattern of self-pity, mind-created imaginations, and negative downward stairs. Really what makes us different from other mammals is our ability to control our thoughts and think for ourselves happiness and shift our unhappy thoughts to a happy feelings and to happy living. We may have made mistakes, but now we can accept it and continue, knowing that we will make a different decision in the future. If we understand this it can be appreciative for the experience. We cannot be both angry and grateful at the same time. We should start counting the blessings and miracles in our lives and if we start exploring for them and we would find more happiness in doing so.

Feeling good about ourselves and showing self-confidence.

Feeling good about ourselves and showing self-confidence boosts our skills potential and capabilities in any areas of work and supports us to become happier. We need to shift our thoughts from being a unhappy person to more strong and positive man.

Also keeping in mind that pushing things to the limit and going beyond what we think is possible for us to get to the next step of being happy. It becomes another key to achieving what we really want to do. We only want happiness and want to lead a happy life.

Even if it may even be relationships and we are finding it difficult to meet someone where we are actually interested in, we need not wait because it usually doesn't come to us by own, we must stand up to get help from any learned fellow. One of the most important things while doing all of this is to be happy about what we are doing, thus we ought to have a successful goal setting our lifestyle with a happy attitude. We may or may not be able to solve the problem of unhappiness that lies within us, but at least knowing that we are taking positive steps that can help us improve our happiness. It will not be easy, of course, for us and it may be like suffering a chronic disease thus we must balance ourselves as "being happy" with an understanding that the reality is, it is going to be an ongoing battle for our own survival. Depression will undermine even the strongest of wills, need help to maintain or at least be reminded of a happy outlook and happiness that is prevailing within us. Counseling, psychotherapy, and the right combination of medication will play a crucial role in helping to keep us from sinking into that very dark place that is the essence of depression and unhappiness. Be patient, but don't look for miracles. It may be that we will need the help of professionals throughout our lives to maintain a generally even keel. If one could "will away" depression, there would be no need of doctors or drugs. What we can do is understand why we feel like we do, and explain to our counselors that we wish it were that easy, and that we appreciate our concern towards being happy persons. Shifting our thoughts enables us to the right path of our happiness and thinking in its direction of positivity can make us to lead a very happy life.

CHAPTER 25

THINK POSITVEAND START HAPPY LIVING

Even when you are facing challenges, it is important to stay open to laughter and humor. Sometimes, simply recognizing the potential humor in a situation can lessen your stress and brighten your outlook. Seeking out sources of humor such as watching a funny sitcom or reading jokes online can help you think more positive thoughts. We need to know and realize that nobody is perfect or flawless. If we try to change the way we look, talk and behave just to please others, and show our pride we will gradually become such a person that we ourselves won't recognize each other and would start and create unnecessary worries within us and our surrounding without being positive and will not start to live happily. We ought to stop worrying over unnecessary things be positive and live without fear happily. As a result, negative thoughts can creep into your mind. While you know that thinking positively is better for your state of mind, you might be surprised to learn that it can also be good for your health. We need to understand that what people think of us is their concern, and not ours. If they think about us to be, too reticent or proud, it's really not our business. If every time we happen to meet some new fellows, we may wonder and imagine as what they think of us, and with this feeling in us we will never be able to live a trouble-free and hassle free life. We are bound to fall into the trap of unnecessary worries denying us the startup of new and the happy living life. We must think rationally. Is it in our hands or can we control what others think about us?

Simply we need to ignore them If we cannot, and live our lives the way we want to and find the ways to leave worries aside and start living a happy life. Let us make our way to happy living.

Positive Thinking with Positive Attitudes.

Positive thinking is not about putting on a pair of rose-colored glasses and ignoring all the negative things you will encounter in life. That approach can be just as devastating as ignoring the positive and only focusing on the negative. Balance, with a healthy dose of realism, is the key. It is a well-known fact that attitude decides how a natives or persons copes up with the day to day events of life. Attitude is what a influence a person's reaction to a situation in life is. It sets the emotional undertone for a person to his likes or dislikes a situation even before he is acquainted with it. Positive attitude is a quality that is second to none in a human being. Though we attach so much importance to this attitude, as we grow into teenage and adult years we find ourselves becoming ungrateful or taking things for granted. We lose touch with the very same qualities that we instill in our children. We take for granted our life, our health, our families, the people in our lives, the things that our loved ones do for us to make our lives easier and things that we possess. The attitude of positive speaks a lot about a person. It denotes about changing negative attitudes and making positive thinking a positive attitude a good habit. Thinking positively and a positive attitude help us to appreciate and value ourselves, our potential and all that we have. It ensures that we do not take our abilities for granted. It makes us look at ourselves as special people with a special set of abilities and potential. It banishes the feelings of inadequacy and insecurity that arises from unfair comparisons with others.

It helps us to appreciate people for who they are and not magnify what they are not and their little flaws. It drives away prejudice and makes us approach life with an open mind. It predisposes us to react to the daily events of life in a positive manner and help us to look at the brighter side of life. Make us optimistic. It gives hope and helps us look forward to life with anticipation. We need to know that positive thinking takes the focus away from what we don't have, to appreciating and making good use of what we have. It is closely connected to our emotional wellbeing and happiness. We feel loved and at peace with ourselves for a major part of our lives when we make this attitude ours. This adds and helps us to get rid of greed, amenity, bitterness, jealousy, and promotes a healthy and nurturing attitude towards others, which in turn gets reciprocated and we feel the sense of healthy living. We attach so much importance to this attitude of gratitude that when our children fail to thank someone, we insist that they do it. That is what is needed to be avoided from time to time. We expect this in return from others when we help them or give them a gift. We call a person discourteous and rude when they do not say thank us in return.On the face of it we ought to know that a positive is not an attitude of being satisfied and content, that you never want to do anything, anymore. This is an attitude that makes you feel good about who you are, what you do, and what your potentials are. This attitude impels you to utilize all that you are endowed with as a person, to achieve the highest possible goals. When we have this attitude, we are able to work without any external pressure to perform but there is sufficient pressure and motivation from within. The possessing of positive thinking is like any other habit, so we need to follow the routine of habit formation here as well. You will win new friends and admirers without having to impress them or conform to the pressure of doing things their way.

You will be bubbling with life and the joie de vivre. You will be rearing to go and accomplish all you can with your new found confidence. The best part of adopting the 'positive thinking and a positive attitude of gratitude is that, you will be able to enjoy the smallest pleasures of nature with a heightened sense of satisfaction and awe. I can see and watch a beautiful flower and carry that joy in my mind for future enjoyment with a clear positive habit. I can go back to work freshen and can use it as an object to meditate on when I feel stressed. Let us be clear that a positive is not an attitude of being satisfied and content, that you never want to do anything, anymore. This is an attitude that makes you feel good about who you are, what you do, and what your potentials are. This attitude impels you to utilize all that you are endowed with as a person, to achieve the highest possible goals. When we have this attitude, we are able to work without any external pressure to perform but there is sufficient pressure and motivation from within. The habit of positive thinking is like any other habit, so we need to follow the routine of habit formation here as well.

CHAPTER 26

WHAT DO YOU GET OUT OF BEING SAD?

You may feel largely uncomfortable, when worries attack your thoughts and mind which makes worrying about a situation an easier option to get depressed and diffused. While you are consuming more worries you are far too busy to do anything else to fix the real problem and would rather find it hard to get into a smart solution. Thus resulting in a fact that you spend your evenings worrying only without even bothering to find some time to search a new job. You get nothing out of worrying except only to think and cry. Another cause of getting worried is the attachment with which your inner soul gets attracted to. Attachment brings worry. If you have a problem and you come up with the answer, you stop worrying immediately. Our minds can be dishonest, persuading us that we are worrying about something, when our deepest fear is entirely different. No-one likes to admit that they've chosen to worry. The first step is to write down your worries, which will help you make sense of them, and then decide on one small step you can take towards a solution. But to be very true no man in this world is free of obstacles or difficulties. Don't make worry your habit. Break this habit and stop all the negative and panic thoughts provoking your mind all the time. If you can't change the past, but you must not ruin the present by worrying about the future. Joy is what happens to us when we allow ourselves to recognize how good things really are.

When we feel worried and depressed, we need to consciously form a smile on our faces and act upbeat until the happy feeling becomes genuine reality. Feelings of depression and hopelessness and or anger are even tougher to cope with on a consistent basis. When you are worried, you not only hurt yourself, but the limited support systems that are still holding on your mind but making you to get more and more worried and nothing is achieved in terms of success except the re-carnation of worries and worries. Your actions breed confidence and courage. If you want to conquer fear, anger and worry do not sit ideal and just think about it. Let our deep worrying become advance thinking and planning. If you look into your own mind and heart, and you find nothing wrong there, what is there to worry about? Practically nothing what is there to fear about and again nothing? So why worry unnecessarily and make your present and future dark.

CHAPTER 27

STEPS FOR HAPPY LIFE

The secret of successful and happy life lies in keeping ourselves smiling and the character which is the foremost important reason that lies within us. Do not be curious about anything, but in everything, by prayer and petition, with thanksgiving, present your requests to God. Whenever your mind is tempted to jump the fence and start to worry, say this verse aloud or to yourself. You may even have to repeat it over and over again. Am I constantly striving to see the positive in every aspect of my life?. Steps for a successful and happy life. At time we may think that there is no road is left for us from were we can achieve the happiness of our lives. We may also feel that life has become terrible for us to live and we are carrying new hope that someone would come to rescue us. There may be chances that someone who was there with us before might have held on to us when we were on the dark side of the life. We should not forget that happiness in life comes through the doors of positive thoughts; we need to have them first. If one door happen to close, another opens, in the event only when we are confident and optimistic. We have so many reasons to cry and at the same time plenty of reasons to smile as well.

Similarly, happiness does not stand for anything, but is on our way of thinking that how do we keep ourselves happy in life. Failure and disappointment are part of our life. The only thing is that we need to face and solve the problem is by keeping our dreams and hope alive be it a reason that success and happiness will come our way again.

The experience has taught us that we should buy some strength, hope and positivity from our loved ones to help ourselves in such a situation rather than surrendering as life is a precious gift of God and is equipped with full of joy and happiness if we help ourselves in these critical moments we can live with considerable optimism. What if when everything goes wrong and all the doors of happiness are closed our live becomes a silent. It is a quite common and we are aware of a marvelous proverb that Life itself is a stage and we all are the performers, performing different acts assigned to us by our almighty power. We should not forget as to what is in our possession? if it is to fulfill our duties towards our responsibility and do whatever is correct and is allowed by us in our life?. However, despite of all these good thoughts which are embodied to us by the almighty fail to revive these unwanted circumstances that lead us to sorrow and difficulties and a situation where we do not know what is correct and good for us and what is wrong for us. We should always remember that, "Life is there, where there is hope". That single thing that remains in our hands is to find out ways to know how to overcome these worries of our life at that very moment when all doors are closed for us which means that whatever situation is there, we must not give up hope. We must fight because there have been always a chance that with good faith and hard work we can turn the odds in our favor. It is often said that it is very easy to advice but when it comes to us, things go out of our control and we fail to suggest a way out for ourselves.

We fall into the trap of unnecessary worries and elope ourselves with negative thoughts. We feel better when somebody else is facing some difficulty but when it comes to us we fail to gather that faith, will power and the words of strength. It is a common fact that no one in this world is free of obstacles or difficulties.

If all the openings of happiness are shut for us and we have to overcome that and have no way to come out, but to survive lest we must have to learn to swim out of the sorrows because this is what is called life and sorrow free living. There are lot more examples and in many other situations, where we will find that how we could have faced and fought with our sorrows and difficulties of life when there was no hope left in our lives. When the power of will is at the worst and each one of us knows that the one who is gone never comes back. Neither a thousands of words would not be enough to bring him back nor a million tears, because each and every moment, eyes would only shed tears , mind would remain tensed and we would be simply surrounded by worries and the life seems to have been vanished. Life is ever expanding, contraction is death. As commonly said by big saints that the self- seeking man who is looking after his personal comforts and leading a lazy life for himself there would be no room for him even in the hell and he simply have lost the power of his will.

We are quite aware of the fact that faith in oneself is the history of a man and that faith calls the quality of superiority within a person. One cannot do anything without it. We fail only when we do not try very hard to achieve the power and faith within us. As soon as we lose faith, death comes in our way and we are surrounds by all the evils and stupid worries of the world. The secret and history of every successful man is to have, good confidence, faith and strength behind him and that remain the right cause of his single success in life. Unselfishness plays a very vital role in his life. He may not have been perfectly unselfish, yet he was tending towards it. If he had been perfectly unselfish, he would have been as great a success. The degree of unselfishness marks the degree of success everywhere and he leads to be successful man without fear worries and selfishness.

There are quite a number of reasons to believe that for a successful and happy life the mystery surrounding it lies in our interests, and good memory which is the basis of our interest, power of desire and aim, keeping ourselves smiling and the doubt free character which is the foremost important reason for a successful and happy life. If we possess one solid unselfish and doubt free character within ourselves we would be quite happy and successful.

The love for God and worshipping God adds to one common thing the immense faith in Him. There may be different beliefs and ways to worship God in different communities, places and religions, but one thing remains the same and that is the Love of God for all of us. Our world is full of odds and evens, happiness and sorrows, fulfilment and emptiness. And these are all created by the Almighty. However, the most beautiful Gift of God, is Human, which is such a mystery driven by Him which could hardly be defined or explained in depth.

We know that life cannot be foreseen. Life is not a bed of roses. Life is a battle field and not a bed of roses as every man on earth has to struggle very hard in making his life happy. If aim of our life is to stay happy and let others to be happy, we will be happy and remembered by all. But no one will actually remember us for the wealth we have gained, or success we have achieved. I have no aim in life. Summary living with no purpose in life is just like a feather moving towards the wind. Both career and purpose are different issues but it is equally important to understand the value of these things which would ultimately add spicy flavor to your living. Innovation at work place is what is it necessary how well we judge our work, how good we like and enjoy it. If we take our work as a stiff challenge and as learning every day, then we would start loving it and giving our best.

However, if we just work for the sake of then nothing is realized and we do not remain happy in life. Life is such a special gift of Almighty and it is not gifted by Him to use it the way we like or love to. The actual path shown by Him needs to be followed by us for us to reach the peak of betterment every moment. We need to have some positive attitude to look at it comfortably but at the same time having a positive mental attitude does not mean banishing all negative thoughts and people from your life. The same is true with thoughts.

When we go to field with negative thoughts, we banish one and another one arises. Therefore creation of positivity in life is utmost necessary to enjoy the special gift of God to us. Now let's us imagine that we are not feeling at our best today, and we are having thoughts that could be classified as negative. We shouldn't be thinking such negative thoughts. We don't like the negative thoughts. We ought to know that negative thoughts are stressful, demoralizing and depressing. We shouldn't aim to have negative thoughts at all. Often we feel uncomfortable because we think we have to say or do something in response to another person's words. When we find ourselves thinking this way, it helps enormously to take a few moments to check inside and notice what we are feeling. We are deeply depressed that negativity has governed us and has taken a deep root in our minds.

If we want to live a positive, joyful life, we must not be surrounded by negative people who don't encourage our happiness. As a negative person, we ought to get attracted too negative people only. Only when we decide to make the change to live a more positive life, we have to get rid of our lives of the most negative influences in it.

We are quite aware of the fact that no one is perfect and perfection isn't the goal when it comes to positivity but there were people in our lives who were consistently negative, who constantly bring us down, we need to stop spending so much time with them. We can very well imagine; it is not easy for us to get away from these negative people. It can hurt us to keep distance from people even when you know they aren't good for us and for our current lifestyle. In addition to removing negative influences from them, we also have to get rid of some of our own negative behaviors, such as the drug and alcohol abuse. We need to take some concrete steps and examine which behaviors are good for us and which were not harmful. What we need is to learn to focus on the positive things, such as working on positive activities and cultivating new, positive relationships. We must let go of the negative ones. This process may be not easy to live a positive life when negative people and behaviors continually pull us down. In every situation or in every person there is something good. Most of the time it's not easy to find the positive qualities but we have to look hard to discover positivity in them. Now, when we are faced with a difficult or challenging situation, we need to think and talk to ourselves and console our mind, no matter how terrible the situation might seem, we can always find something good if we take the time to think about it. It is quite obvious that anything good and bad is learning experience so, at the very least, we must learn from bad experiences. However, there's usually even more to it than that. If you really take some time to have a look at it, we would find something good, something genuinely positive, about every person or situation. Once we start thinking more positively, we will realize that we had to reinforce these thoughts and behaviors within ourselves so that we could stick to it. As with any sort of training, the more we practice, the better we get to be positive.

The best and easiest way to do this is to be positive when it comes to who we are. We need to speak to ourselves that we are awesome. And we have done a good job at work thus creating positivity within us. We need to be honest with ourselves, and we need to do our best to look for the good. And, whatever we do, we must not focus on the negative. It is alright not to like everything about ourselves, but don't focus on what we don't like. We have all the positive attributes, and it's up to us to remind ourselves of them every day. Not only do we need to be positive with ourselves for this multiple action to take effect, but we need to be more positive with others. We have to share our wealth of positivity with the people of the world. The best way is to be nice with other people, no matter what. Tell them that they look nice today. Appreciate their job and tell them that have done a great job on that assignment. Be positive and tell your elder or your kids how much you love them and how great they are. When someone is feeling down, do what we need to do is to cheer him or her up. Do send them gifts nice flower and glow them with nice notes.

CHAPTER 28

WHAT DO YOU GET OUTOF BEING NOT HAPPY?

If you are interested in getting more success and happiness within you, focus on all the ways as if you have already attained success. You need to focus on the thing and create a happy live within you. If you want love and affection, focus on all the people and the abundance of love that you have to give to them. If we want to have greater health, focus on all the ways that we are healthy, thus creating and delivering a good life within you. You need to admit that there are problems that you cannot change. But you can change the way of your thinking if you identify the main reason of the problem. And if you acknowledge the facts, that you have been negative or inactive in finding a solution to the problem, probably this will make it easier for you to become positive thus creating a new lease of life within you. It will make your life easier to lead a good and sweet life.

You must try to make goals

You must try to make goals. Making goals can give you a more positive outlook on life. People often tend to get bored with life and get the feeling that they are stuck to negative things which the result they often get the feeling of being depressed. Setting a direction for yourself and a goal would surely help you to move forward.

Mental attitude that can bring you peace and happiness

If you expecting to succeed, and are not afraid of failure, you have the best chance of staying positive and can create a very positive life within you. When you, or any of your associates, are tempted to worry about a problem, write out the solution and a definite answer to it. This helps a positive feeling to generate within you making you very positive to have a good living. Another thing you need to understand is that there are several ways to cultivate a mental attitude that can bring you peace and happiness and can carnage a good life within you. More of it if you fill your mind with thoughts of peace, courage, health, and hope, your life will be easy to live. You would get a happy feeling of life and mind if you let yourself to forget your own unhappiness, by trying to create a little happiness for others. You are best to yourself and to others.

The first step is to write down your worries

The first step is to write down your worries, which will help you make sense of them, and then decide on one small step you can take towards a solution. But to be very true no man in this world is free of obstacles or difficulties. Don't make worry your habit. Break this habit and stop all the negative and panic thoughts provoking your mind all the time. If you can't change the past, but you must not ruin the present by worrying about the future. Joy is what happens to us when we allow ourselves to recognize how good things really are. When we feel worried and depressed, we need to consciously form a smile on our faces and act upbeat until the happy feeling becomes genuine reality. Happiness is what is needed most.

What makes to lead a happy life is not to get trapped into unnecessary unwanted worries and negative thoughts.

Don't create the feeling of depression and anger.

Feelings of depression and hopelessness and or anger are even tougher to cope with on a consistent basis. When you are worried, you not only hurt yourself, but the limited support systems that are still holding on your mind but making you to get more and more worried and nothing is achieved in terms of success except the re-carnation of worries and worries thus leading you to be unhappy and worried all the time. Your actions breed confidence and courage. If you want to conquer fear, anger and worry do not sit ideal and just think about it. Let our deep worrying become advance thinking and planning. If you look into your own mind and heart, and you find nothing wrong there, what is there to worry about? Practically nothing what is there to fear about and again nothing? So why worry unnecessarily and make your present and future dark. Neglect all those which make your life unhappy.

Why being a negative person?

Why being a negative person and what do you get out of it being a depression dejected and sad man.? Why not turn your thoughts to be a positive person simply it is a question of tilting your mind towards a positive side of thing. See both the aspects of a situation and ways the pros and cons of both the sides and try to abolish the negativity in you. Be positive strong and you will remain happy for ever. We all have different roles that we play in the lives of people we love and care about.

Our actions and how well we play our part has a direct influence on their life, so we better get in there and give our best performance. Tell them with how much you care in the capacity that you're in. At the end of the day, money is just a means to an end. Nothing more. If you're grinding and struggling to make ends meet and buried under piles of debt, that's pretty stressful. Once you have your basic needs met though, more money only makes you happier up to a certain point. Money cannot buy you happiness. You need to generate it yourself. Someone will always be better than you at something, but it does not matter. Be inspired by them, using it to push yourself further, and nothing more. If they can do it, why cannot you?

Are you are interested in getting more happiness?

If you are interested in getting more happiness focus on all the ways as if you have already attained success. You need to focus on the thing and create a live within you. If you want love and affection, focus on all the people and the abundance of love that you have to give to them.

Worrisome thoughts reproduce faster.

Worrisome thoughts reproduce faster so one of the most powerful ways to stop the spiral of worry is simply to disclose the worry too a friend. Practice happy gratitude daily.

Take three minutes at the end of your day to chill and write down a small list of the things that can make you smile, laugh, or that you're glad are a part of your life.

There's something to be grateful about, especially when you look down at that list and realize that a lot of people have it worse off than you do and could use a few of those things. Simply being an optimist will not solve all your problems, but what's the alternative is to keep your mind and heart cool and always have happy and positive feeling and think that life is to live happily. There isn't much sense in being anything else. If you're constantly filling your head with negative thoughts, odds are they'll lead you straight towards negative actions, self-doubt and increase the general happiness of life isn't a cool place to live at all. Think of each setback as a challenge to see the positive, spin the situation back around, making it better than it was before and start living in a good and sweet manner.

What do we get out of unhappiness?

We may feel largely uncomfortable, when worries attack our thoughts and mind. While we are consuming more worries we are far too busy to do anything else to fix the real problem and would rather find it hard to get into a smart solution. Thus resulting in a fact that you spend your evenings worrying only without even bothering to find some time to know its cause We get nothing out of worrying except only to think and cry and become unhappy. We do not get anything out of unhappiness. Another thing is that we may feel largely uncomfortable, when worries attack our thoughts and mind which makes worrying about a situation an easier option to get depressed and diffused. While we are consuming more worries we are far too busy to do anything else to fix the real problem and would rather find it hard to get into a smart solution.

Thus resulting in a fact that we spend our evenings worrying only without even bothering to find some time to search a sweet happiness within us.

Negative thoughts create unnecessary worries

Negative thought which are provoking our mind, about the uncertainties and the negativities, as to what will happen tomorrow creates unnecessary worries and worries are repetitive thoughts associated with feelings of anxiety Whether the worries are about financial crisis, family problems, work, health or any topic of concern, the anxious feelings and negative thoughts produced are always distinctly unpleasant thus making us unhappy all the time. We get nothing being a negative and unhappy man. We must not forget that if we tend to worry they will never rob tomorrow of its sorrows, but will only deny today of its meaning happiness and joys. Negative thoughts only produce worries and worrying is actually a form of superstition and creates false images in our mind and that is the main reason and cause which makes and leads us to this point of imagination. A human being can survive almost anything, as long as he or she sees the end in sight, starts analyzing his positive thoughts and starts analyzing his unhappiness.

We need to fore see the coming trouble first.

We must not forgot that if something bad or good is to happen it is sure to happen, whether we worry or not. Let us put our energy into today and stop worrying about the future and past.

We should not foresee trouble, or worry about what may never happen as past is dead and gone forever and future is uncertain and yet to come. Positive thinking our brave attitude and our courage will ward off everything and bring happiness in our lives. The basic facts we should know about worry. The basic techniques to analyze worry and how to break the worry habit before it breaks us. These are the simple ways where we can concentrate and get rid of worries prevailing in our thoughts, remove all the negativity in our live and start living a positive good and happy life.

Think of good and positive ways of Happy Living.

Annalise positive ways of happy living and get to see the reasons and facts of worry. To avoid reoccurrence of worries, concentrate on prayers as prayers are the best source of remedies of the prevailing worries. Think good ways of living and starting praying. The more you pray, the less you'll panic. The more you worship, the less you worry. There is nothing that wastes the body like worry, and anyone who has any faith in God should need not to worry about anything whatsoever is to happen in future. Positive thinking is the creation of good imagination and good imagination is the creation of sweet and happy living.

Happiness comes with Positive living and sweet thoughts

If you know that the circumstance is beyond your control or power change than revise it to your liking. Just try to put a stop-less order on your worries.

Don't permit little things which become insects of life to ruin your happiness. Co-operate with the inevitable. Decide just how much anxiety a thing may be worth and refuse to give in anymore.

All the happiness is not given in one go it comes slowly and slowly with positive thinking.

Have worry under your control. If your worries center around, pay special attention to remain positive and be happy. Keep yourself happy, treat your worried thoughts as valuable signals. How to keep from worrying about criticism? Simply unjust criticism and think positively and do often discard a bad compliment. It often means that you have aroused jealousy and envy. Let's keep a record of the fool things we have done and stop criticizing ourselves.

Cause of unhappiness is Negative way of living life

The utmost cause of worry is our negative thinking as it leads us to the state of depression. Living will change for the better- If You Think Positive. Our negative thinking and attitude towards suffering and depression becomes very important because it can affect how we cope with suffering when it arises. Depression is nourished by a lifetime of un-grieved and unforgiven causes. Times will change for the better when you change. Worry is a misuse of the imagination. Worry is most often a prideful way of thinking that you have more control over life and its circumstances than you actually do. Positive Thinking leads your way to good and happiness. An art of Good and Happy Living.

Neglect worries keep yourself happy.

Neglect worries keep yourself happy, treat your worried thoughts as valuable signals. These are the fundamental facts you should be familiar about worries. A huge factor to stay happy is to cater your worries around, an important relationship in your life and pay special attention sustaining positive relationships. Worries are there to motivate information gathering and problem-solving. Make your mind firm and do come to a positive decision as come what we will not allow the worries to entire our mind and soul.

What if we just acted like everything was easy?

Once a decision is carefully reached we should get busy carrying out our decisions and should not bother about all the anxieties that are about to come. When we, or any of our colleagues or associates, are about to worry about a problem, we must write it out and think positively of the questions. Instead of worrying about what people say of you, why not spend time trying to accomplish something they will admire. What if we just acted like everything was easy? How would your life be different if you stopped worrying about things we can't control and started focusing on the things we can? Let today be the day. Free yourself from fruitless worry, seize the day and take effective action on things you can change. We would change ourselves for the betterment if we start thinking in positive terms. Positive thinking is what is required of us and simply worrying about the future things or as to what will happen in the next moment will certainly deprive us of good and happy living that we are about gather or get in the next hour.

Another cause of getting worried or unhappy is the attachment

Attachment brings worry. If you have a problem and you come up with the answer, you stop worrying immediately. Our minds can be dishonest, persuading us that we are worrying about something, when our deepest fear is entirely different. No-one likes to admit that they've chosen to worry. The first step is to write down your worries, which will help you make sense of them, and then decide on one small step you can take towards a solution.

But to be very true no man in this world is free of obstacles or difficulties. Don't make worry your habit. Break this habit and stop all the negative and panic thoughts provoking your mind all the time if you want to remain a happy person and lead a happy good and sweet life. Feelings of depression and angry are even tougher to cope with on a consistent basis. When you are worried, you not only hurt yourself, but the limited support systems that are still holding on your mind making you to get more and more worried and nothing is achieved in terms of success except the re-carnation of worries and worries Joy is what happens to us when we allow ourselves to recognize how good things really are.

Practically nothing what is there to fear about?

So why worry unnecessarily and make your present and future dark. Why being a negative person and what do you get out of it being a depression dejected and sad man.?

Why not turn your thoughts to be a positive person simply it is a question of tilting your mind towards a positive side of thing. See both the aspects of a situation and ways the pros and cons of both the sides and try to abolish the negativity in you. You will surely be a happy man.

Think of the best the best is sure to happen

Think of the best the best is sure to happen and if you think of the worst the worst will come. Better come forward wake up and think positive first. Positive persons always succeed in life whatever be the circumstances and the negative often dig a death trap for themselves. So why be a negative person why you have all the qualities of being a positive man. Surround yourself with friends and people that are better than you in areas that you want to improve in. Learn from them, let them push you out of your comfort zone and it's only a matter of time before you level up as well. Happiness is neither virtue nor pleasure nor this thing nor that but simply growth. We are happy when we are growing.

CHAPTER 29

MAKE YOUR WAY TO HAPPY LIVING

We need to learn a lesson from every situation. No matter how difficult the situation may appear. We should recognize the beautiful lessons waiting to be discovered. Sometimes lessons may prove to be expensive and costly, but every problem is a learning experience in disguise. We need to be conscious of our thoughts, especially, when life just isn't going our way. The moment we see that we are diving into frustration, agony, sorrow or low self –esteem we must shift our thoughts, by thinking about something completely different and unrelated. You are essentially trying to cultivate a new habit here, the secret of successful and happy life lies in keeping ourselves smiling and the character which is the foremost important reason that lies within us. Whenever your mind is tempted to jump the fence and start to worry, say this verse aloud or to yourself. You may even have to repeat it over and over again. Am I constantly striving to see the positive in every aspect of my life? Steps for a successful and happy life.

MAKE YOUR WAY TO HAPPY LIVING

We need to believe that a happy living is a matter of our choice. This step is hard to take. People are either positive or negative. They tend to blame their negativity on all kinds of outside forces fate, experiences, parents, relationship, but never really stopped to think that they could choose to be happy. Piercing ourselves that happiness is a choice has been one of the greatest things we have ever done for ourselves.

Now when we find ourselves in a bad situation, we know that it is up to us to find the good, to be happy regardless of what is happening around us. We should no longer point fingers and place blame to anyone else. We need to realize that everything happens how it happens, and it is up to us to choose how we want to feel about it. We need to be in control of our attitude and happiness, and no one can take that away this from us.

Unhappiness is contagious and spreads like fire.

It not only does its affect anyone, but it spreads to everyone who ever comes in contact with it or whoever they interact with. When only the negative perspective is in focus, the resolution process is impeded. Eliminating unhappiness, or rather, being happy is a mindset that can be found at any moment, and which can be turned into a habit. If we want to live a happy, joyful life, we must not be surrounded by negative people who don't encourage our happiness. As a negative person, we ought to get attracted to negative people only. Only when we decide to make the change to live a more positive and happy life, we have to get rid of our lives of the most negative influences in it. We are quite aware of the fact that no one is perfect and perfection is not the goal when it comes to positivity but there were people in our lives who were consistently negative, who constantly bring us down, we need to stop spending so much time with them. We can very well imagine, it is not easy for us to get away from these unhappy people. It can hurt us to keep distance from people even when you know they are not good for us and for our current lifestyle.

In addition to removing negative influences from them, we also have to get rid of some of our own negative behaviors, such as the drug and alcohol abuse. We need to take some concrete steps and examine which behaviors are good for us and which were not harmful. What we need is to learn to focus on the happy things, such as working on positive activities and cultivating new, positive relationships. We must let go of the negative ones. This process may be not easy to live a positive life when negative people and behaviors continually pull us down. We need to discard all of them to lead a happy and sweet life. An art of sweet living lies below us we have only to recognize it.

Look For Sweet Living in Life

The real test of any one is to remain happy whenever some challenges become difficult. Remaining happy keeps our mind in the right state of balance and often opens resolutions to the problems at hand. We must throw away the unhappiness in us and opt for being a very positive person. In every situation or in every person there is something good. Most of the time it's not easy to find the happiness qualities but we have to look hard to discover happiness in them. Now, when we are faced with a difficult or challenging situation, we need to think and talk to ourselves and console our mind, no matter how terrible the situation might seem, we can always find something good if we take the time to think about it. It is quite obvious that anything good and bad is learning experience so, at the very least, we must learn from bad experiences. However, there is usually even more to it than that.

If you really take some time to have a look at it, we would find something good, something genuinely happy, about every person or situation. We must look for sweet living in life

Get Sweet feeling in your life

Once we start thinking more in a happy manner, we will realize that we had to reinforce these thoughts and behaviors within ourselves so that we could stick to it. As with any sort of training, the more we practice, the better we get to be happy. The best and easiest way to do this is to be happy when it comes to who we are. We need to speak to ourselves that we are awesome. And we have done a good job at work thus creating happiness within us. We need to be honest with ourselves, and we need to do our best to look for the good. And, whatever we do, we must not focus on the negative. It is alright not to like everything about ourselves, but don not focus on what we do not like. We have all to get the sweet feeling in our lives, and it is up to us to remind ourselves of them every day.

Share sweet and happy thoughts

Not only do we need to be happy with ourselves for this multiple action to take effect, but we need to be more happy with others too.We have to share our wealth of happiness with the people of the world. The best way is to be nice with other people and to make them happy, no matter what the matter is. Tell them that they look nice today. What is required is that we never wanted to see the good in ourselves and, therefore, didn't want to see it in others also.

We must not be critical and condescending rather we must be encouraging and supportive. We should not try to treat others as we would like to be treated, but also try to consider how we would like to be treated. This will strangle the pattern of self-pity, mind-created imaginations, and negative downward stairs. Really what makes us different from other mammals is our ability to control our thoughts and think for ourselves happiness and shift our unhappy thoughts to a happy feelings and to happy living. We may have made mistakes, but now we can accept it and continue, knowing that we will make a different decision in the future.

If we understand this it can be appreciative for the experience. We cannot be both angry and grateful at the same time. We should start counting the blessings and miracles in our lives and if we start exploring for them and we would find more happiness in doing so.

Feeling good about ourselves and showing self-confidence.

Feeling good about ourselves and showing self-confidence boosts our skills potential and capabilities in any areas of work and supports us to become happier. We need to shift our thoughts from being a unhappy person to more strong and positive man.

lso keeping in mind that pushing things to the limit and going beyond what we think is possible for us to get to the next step of being happy. It becomes another key to achieving what we really want to do.

We only want happiness and want to lead a happy life. Even if it may even be relationships and we are finding it difficult to meet someone where we are actually interested in, we need not wait because it usually doesn't come to us by own, we must stand up to get help from any learned fellow. One of the most important things while doing all of this is to be happy about what we are doing, thus we ought to have a successful goal setting our lifestyle with a happy attitude.

We may or may not be able to solve the problem of unhappiness that lies within us, but at least knowing that we are taking positive steps that can help us improve our happiness. It will not be easy, of course, for us and it may be like suffering a chronic disease thus we must balance ourselves as "being happy" with an understanding that the reality is, it is going to be an ongoing battle for our own survival.

Depression will undermine even the strongest of wills, need help to maintain or at least be reminded of a happy outlook and happiness that is prevailing within us. Counseling, psychotherapy, and the right combination of medication will play a crucial role in helping to keep us from sinking into that very dark place that is the essence of depression and unhappiness.

Be patient, but don't look for miracles. It may be that we will need the help of professionals throughout our lives to maintain a generally even keel. If one could "will away" depression, there would be no need of doctors or drugs.

What we can do is understand why we feel like we do, and explain to our counselors that we wish it were that easy, and that we appreciate our concern towards being happy persons.

Shifting our thoughts enables us to the right path of our happiness and thinking in its direction of positivity can make us to lead a very happy life.Take care of your health Eat well do plenty of exercise and do not skip meals It is a known fact that Physical exercise is known to stimulate our veins and get to strengthen our minds that lift depression and anxiety so we need to walk, swim, run or whatever we like doing best. Those who create or those who do well on the worst scenario, give themselves worry and stress, tend to be devastated. If we cannot get some sunshine, we can always lighten up our rooms with brighter lights. We can have lunch outside the office. Take frequent walks instead of driving our cars over short distances. No man is indispensable. First of all our circle of friends is always there to give us some moral support. Spending time and engaging ourselves in worthwhile activities could give us a very enjoyable and satisfying feeling. Nothing feels better than having group support. Good friends are quite important and their company generally lightened up our spirits. To get to know and to find such friends we simply have to be friendly with ourselves, and then the friendships will naturally follow us. We need to understand the power of touch and support and we have not to underestimate it strength and support. Don't we feel so good when someone pats us on our back and gives us some words of encouragement during your most challenging times and difficult times?

Just hug or embrace someone someday you will see that you have almost changed his life. Get intimate with him and try to establish close ties with his family and friends. The love and care expressed by you will tremendously boost him and well as your immune system and fury of worry will be diminished for all. In our lives storms may come and go in the form of reversals, but if we have the power and foundation of inner fulfillment and if we deal with it with a very clear practical mind these storms will not kill us or will not disrupt us. There could be numberless reasons for which we keep on worrying. We may be worried about our health, wealth, loved ones, friends, the happening f yesterday and the follow happenings of tomorrow, the environment or the world politics, but these can be dealt with firm mind and fearless worry if we generate within ourselves the power of enlightenment within ourselves.

CHAPTER 30

BE HAPPY AND ENJOY YOUR LIFE

We need to remember that as we possibly as we can we should make it a point to eat a more balanced, and healthy diet even though we may very little money left with us. We have intake of lot of greens vegetables and with variety of fruit and nuts which are all super healthy food for us, and which are less expensive than meats, cheeses, and processed foods! Their nitrifying value will energize and elevate our body, and knowing this that we are treating ourselves will surely refresh our minds. If we look for rich food rich in vitamins and other useful ingredients which include nuts, soya beans and fatty fish we would get more nutrition value. We must cut back on the caffeine drinks, alcohol. We don't have to quit, but reducing the intake of them will help reduce anxiety and stress from time to time. Exercise is one of health sport that our body needs most. It may be yoga, cross training, or even a simple walking in the park. This helps keeping our body active and will also help to grow our outlook. If we make it hobby we would enjoy the most. Whether its art, photography, music focusing on something other than the worry factor it will give our mind some good atmosphere to breathe off and would generate a good behavior within us. The other refreshing factor is naturally our sleep. We need not be reminded of this. Our body is probably begging us for it when we are in the middle of hard times. We may be drawn to maintain good sleeping habits. Maintain a consistent sleep schedule, but allow yourself some leeway. If we sleep peacefully let our body get about 8 hours of sleep we get the best results. If you're just starting to have those thoughts, speak to your physician or your therapist.

They may prescribe something to help steer you back to the center, emotionally. It may be the act of talking about it is therapeutic enough, but don't assume that. Leave that call to the professionals. Having goals which are set again and again after each one is achieved will give you a mindset or target to strive for which leads to success, with success becomes natural positive attitude. With all costiveness, goals and success builds a higher potential and belief within yourself. Setting realistic goals that you know you can achieve by staying positive is a great beginning to success. Your attitude around your friends, family and public people really tells them who you are, being positive instead of negative makes an excellent first impression on anybody. Positive means to be absolute, clear-cut, definite, forward-looking and expressively firm with a decision. Having a positive attitude toward something means you are willing to commit and do the work without complaint, which leads to goals. You realize that what appears negative today will change tomorrow. Nothing stays the same. Whether you are positive or negative, the situation does not change. So, we mind as well be positive. As with any habit, the habit of remaining positive in all situations takes practice and a commitment to yourself to take control. But start small, start paying attention to your emotions, start by wanting to change. Don't hold onto anything that bothers your mind. It can only hurt your health and it won't help your problems at all. The people that live the longest in this world do not hold grudges or hold onto negative feelings. Visualize your worries on a large chalkboard in your mind. Watch yourself take a big eraser and erase the problems. Every time the thoughts come back into your head, see yourself with the eraser again. Therefore do not worry about tomorrow, for tomorrow will worry about itself. Each day has enough trouble of its own.

Do not anticipate trouble, or worry about what may never happen. Keep in the sunlight. Imagine every day to be the last of a life surrounded with hopes, cares, anger and fear. The hours that come unexpectedly will be much the more grateful. The mind that is anxious about future events is miserable. Present fears are less than horrible imaginings. Let us be of good cheer, remembering that the misfortunes hardest to bear are those that never happen, focus on the positive aspects of their lives, rather than on the negative setbacks. "Feeling confident affects the way we perceive our situations and how we decide to manage them. Don't waste your life in doubts and fears: spend yourself on the work before you, well assured that the right performance of this hour's duties will be the best preparation for the hours or ages that follow it. It is not work that kills men, it is worry. Work is healthy; you can hardly put more on a man than he can bear. But worry is rust upon the blade. It is not movement that destroys the machinery, but friction. Never let life's hardships disturb you ... no one can avoid problems, not even saints or sages. As with any habit, the habit of remaining positive in all situations takes practice and a commitment to yourself to take control. Life is what you make it, so make it a happy one!!

CHAPTER 31

OUR OTHER PUBLICATION

ARE ON SALE

”MICROSCOPY OF ASTROLOGY”

“MICROSCOPY OF NUMEROLOGY”

“MICROSCOPY OF REMEDIES”

MICROSCOPY OF HAPPY LIVING

MICROSCOPY OF TRANSITING PLANETS

CHAPTER 32

OUR CONTACT ADDRESS

PLEASE SEND YOUR QUERIES TO:

BALDEV BHATIA

CONSULTANT-NUMEROLOGY-ASTROLOGY

C-63, FIRST FLOOR

MALVIYA NAGAR

NEW DELHI-110017

INDIA

TEL NO 919810075249

TEL NO 91 11 26686856

TEL NO 91 7503280786

TEL NO 91 7702735880

CHAPTER 33

OUR MOST SOUGHT WEB SITES

HTTP://WWW.ASTROLOGYBB.COM

HTTP://WWW.BBASTROLOGY.COM

HTTP://WWW.BALDEVBHATIA.COM

HTTP://WWW.BALDEVBHATIA.US

HTTP://WWW.BALDEVBHATIA.ORG

HTTP://WWW.BALDEVBHATIA.INFO

HTTP://WWW.BALDEVBHATIA.NET

HTTP://WWW.BALDEVBHATIA.BIZ

HTTP://WWW.BALDEVBHATIA.IN

CHAPTER 34

SPECIAL NOTE

FROM THE AUTHOR BALDEV BHATIA

THANK YOU FOR READING MY BOOK

MY SINCERE PRAYERS

FOR ALL MY READERS

"GOD BLESS YOU ALL"

"ANY ONE WHO READS AND KEEPS THIS BOOK AS HOLY MANUSCRIPT, GOD IS SURE TO BLESS HIM, WITH ALL THE PEACE, HAPPINESS, WEALTH, HEALTH AND PROSPERITY OF THIS UNIVERSE"

BALDEV BHATIA